SpringerBriefs in Education

CW01095228

Key Thinkers in Education

Series editor

Paul Gibbs, London, UK

This briefs series publishes compact (50 to 125 pages) refereed monographs under the editorial supervision of the Advisory Editor, Professor Paul Gibbs, Middlesex University, Nicosia, Cyprus. Each volume in the series provides a concise introduction to the life and work of a key thinker in education and allows readers to get acquainted with their major contributions to educational theory and/or practice in a fast and easy way.

More information about this series at http://www.springer.com/series/10197

Stephen J. Ball

Foucault as Educator

 Springer

Stephen J. Ball
Department of Humanities and Social
   Sciences
Institute of Education University of London
London
UK

ISSN 2211-1921   ISSN 2211-193X   (electronic)
SpringerBriefs in Education
ISSN 2211-937X   ISSN 2211-9388   (electronic)
SpringerBriefs on Key Thinkers in Education
ISBN 978-3-319-50300-4   ISBN 978-3-319-50302-8   (eBook)
DOI 10.1007/978-3-319-50302-8

Library of Congress Control Number: 2016959182

Printed on acid-free paper

This Springer imprint is published by Springer Nature
The registered company is Springer International Publishing AG
The registered company address is: Gewerbestrasse 11, 6330 Cham, Switzerland

Acknowledgements

There are a lot of people who have directly or indirectly made it possible for me to write this book. Foremost among them is Trinidad, without whom it would never have been finished.

I am also grateful for comments and support from Ansgar Allan, Patrick Bailey, Paul Gibbs, Alex Moore, Antonio Olmedo, Roger Slee, Terry Wrigley, my research student seminar and participants at Foucault @ 90, UWS and very especially I am indebted to Carolina Junemann.

Contents

Abstract

Michel Foucault is a starting point or a set of starting points for this book, not its subject. It consists of a set of improvisations, drawing on Foucault's ideas, that address what the idea of Foucault as Educator might mean in practice, or in relation to practices. It presages specifically the outline of an aesthetics of the self, which Foucault began to address in his later works, as a form of self-education or self-formation. That is, the possibility of 'becoming someone else that you were not'. It is an attempt to begin to envision education as an ethos of transgression and aesthetic self-fashioning. **The point then of the book is not to rehearse Foucault but to consider some ways in which Foucault can be useful; what can we do with Foucault in our educational present that will enable us to think about education differently?**

Keywords Foucault · Education · Critique · Self-formation · Transgression · Refusal

Introduction

Each of my works is a part of my own biography. For one or other reason I had occasion to feel and live those things (Foucault 1988, p. 11)

A couple of years ago I wrote a book exploring how Foucault's tool box of concepts, methods and perspectives might be used in the sociology of education to think differently about how we problematise, research and make sense of education. I began that book by asking whether we needed another Foucault book. There were many such books then, there are even more now. As I begin to write another Foucault book that question is even more pressing. Has not enough been said? Of course, given you are reading this, I have an answer, although I am not sure how convincing an answer it is. I described the previous book as a 'Foucault book', it was not a book *about* Foucault, it was a book about what we might do with Foucault—the ways in which, as he said himself, he might be useful. I am not sure the same can be said about this book. Given the title it is obviously in part *about* Foucault but I am going to deploy the title in a number of ways to think about what Foucault can tell us about education, about the process of education and about what it means to be educated. At times, particularly in the third section of the book, I may be putting words in his mouth. As Allen (2014) puts it, whilst there must be sustained sensitivity to his work and ethos, 'all usages of Foucault must remain partial: those who adopt Foucault can only deform him. This should be done without regret, for, as Nietzsche would say, "one repays a teacher badly if one remains only a pupil"'. So in Chap. 3 I am going to see what might be meant, for the possibilities of education, by what Foucault says about subjectivity and self-formation. In an often quoted exchange, Jana Sawicki describes her encounter with Foucault at a seminar in Vermont in 1983. She explained that she had just finished writing a dissertation based on his critique of humanism. 'Not surprisingly, he responded with some embarrassment and much seriousness. He suggested that I not spend energy talking about him and, instead, do what he was doing, namely, write genealogies' (Sawicki 1991, p. 15). In another sense this book is an exercise in what Foucault called *self writing*, as he says, describing the *hupomnemata*, books used 'as guides for conduct' in ancient Greece: 'Through the interplay of selected readings and assimilative writing, one should be able to form an identity through which a whole spiritual[1] genealogy can be read' (Foucault, nd.). When I speak about Foucault to audiences interested in education, using Foucault's tools of critique, I am always asked—'so what should we do?'. I often reply in Foucault's words that 'it is not for me to tell you what you should do'. Well, while that remains true I feel the ethical weight of the need for a different kind of reply, even if just for my own benefit. So this book is about what we might do about education if we follow the lines of flight indicated by Foucault, and concomitantly it is also about 'the arts of myself' and the aesthetics of my own existence.

To some extent I am going to fashion the book around the tensions, shifts, ruptures, call them what you will, in Foucault's work, that involve his transition from a theorist of oppressions to a theorist of freedoms. However, as he and many others have said, if we read carefully there may be no such transition, rather just different ways of addressing the problem of the history of the ways in which we have been made subjects. And as he also asserted, more or less throughout his work, we are always freer than we think. Both the limitations of a transitions perspective on Foucault's work, and something of the dialectic I am trying to invoke, making limits visible and intolerable and thus opening up the possibility of thinking, and thinking ourselves, differently, are nicely pointed up in this quotation. He argues that the enlightenment should:

> be conceived as an attitude, an ethos, a philosophical life in which the critique of what we are is at one and the same time the historical analysis of the limits that are imposed on us and an experiment with the possibility of going beyond them. Foucault (Foucault 1997, p. 132).

This book is an exercise in finding my own limits and limitations and going beyond them. That is, as an educator, of sorts, I must confront the impossibility of my role and at the same time the possibility of being something else. As a writer I must confront my failings—the failure to grasp and convey what Foucault may have had to say about education, the failure to rid myself of modernist conceits. The more Foucault I read, and the more I read about Foucault, the less I think I understand him, but the more I understand myself and what I am. The book then puts myself under revision—as an *impossible subject*, a Foucauldian educator in a neoliberal university, a human scientist and modernist.

Having said all that, let me make one thing very clear. This book does not attempt any kind of textual interrogation of Foucault or seek to make claims about what Foucault 'actually' was or meant. There is now plenty of work of that kind. In particular at the moment a body of writing that combs Foucault's lectures for traces of neoliberal affinity. The intellectualist tradition of Foucault studies, or at least

---

[1]Foucault wrote about what he called political spirituality, This occurs he says, when people willfully—meaning 'with alertness to the creative dimensions of their project'—seek a new way to establish a regime of truth and a regime of self-governance, each by and through the other. It is putting into question one's style of existence and a process of founding, un-founding, re-founding, creating—of beginnings (see Chap. 3).

IMPOSSIBLE
SUBJECTS .

some parts of it, it seems to me, fails to engage with or recognise key aspects of Foucault's method—and indeed fails to recognise his work as method, treating it instead as a form of traditional philosophy.

> ... The need to interpret Foucault sits ill with his known desire to escape interpretive categories ... interpreting Foucault is guaranteed to distort his thought ... because Foucault's work is at root ad hoc, fragmentary and incomplete ... Foucault is not a hedgehog but a fox (Gutting 1994, p. 1–2).

Textual analysis is self-defeating, it both treats the lectures as closed and finished and coherent texts, which is wrong, and ignores the style and nature of Foucault's intellectual project; as he put it: 'I don't feel that it is necessary to know exactly what I am. The main interest in life and work is to become someone else that you were not in the beginning' (Martin et al. 1998, p. 9). Foucault's attempts at anonymity and the avoidance of fixity in his writings, is fundamentally related to the artistry of his own self-invention, it is a matter of style, it is ethical and political rather than intellectual. He was constantly seeking to avoid the austere gaze of those who sift through his words in order to establish some essential Foucault. Gutting underlines this and Foucault's specificity and marginality: 'Each of Foucault's books strikes a specific tone that is muffled and distorted if we insist on harmonising it with his other books' (1994, p. 3). His work is often inconsistent, sometimes imprecise, always contrarian. To ignore that is to miss a great deal of the point of Foucault. It is worth paying attention to the opening sections of Foucault's lecture series to get a proper sense of the role and purpose of these lectures in his philosophical practice. Ultimately it is the method that is important not the generality of the analysis as a broad historical account of a period. Again as Gutting puts it: it is 'less risky and even more profitable to regard Foucault as an intellectual artisan, someone who over the years constructed a variety of artifacts, the intellectual equivalents of the material objects created by a skilled goldsmith or cabinetmaker' (1994, p.6).

Foucault's statement, 'The main interest in life and work is to become someone else that you were not in the beginning' is important here in two senses. First, for the purposes of this book Foucault is a starting point, or a set of starting points, not a subject. The three sections, particularly the first and third, are a set of improvisations, drawing on Foucault's ideas, that address what the idea of *Foucault as Educator* might mean in practice, or in relation to practices. Second, it presages specifically the outline of an aesthetics of the self, which Foucault began to address in his later works, as a form of self-education or self-formation, which is the focus of Chap. 3. That is, the possibility of 'becoming someone else that you were not'. It is an attempt to begin to envision education as an ethos of transgression and aesthetic self-fashioning. 'Couldn't everyone's life become a work of art?' he declared in a 1983 interview with Hubert Dreyfus. This addresses the problem of how to live, how to relate to one's self and to others. This is no a lonely self reflection but practical work with and in relation to others on how we conduct ourselves in the social world.

The point then of the book is not to rehearse Foucault but to consider some ways in which Foucault can be useful; what can we do with Foucault in our educational present that will enable us to think about education differently?

Rather than seeking to tame or defame or re-modernise Foucault I hope to take up his invitation to use his provocations to think with. As Ewald and Fontana put it in the Introduction to the *Birth of Biopolitics* Lectures (Foucault 2010a, p. xiv) 'Foucault approached his teaching as a researcher: explorations for a future book as well as an invitation to possible future researchers'. This again has some relevance to the question of Foucault as Educator. What I am suggesting is that part of what we might learn from Foucault would draw on the form and style of his scholarly and philosophical practice and much as the content of his lectures and writing. In that sense also this book is not primarily *about* Foucault, it is about his legacy of practice.

What might we learn from Foucault? First, for example, his constant use of paradox as an empirical and analytic device.

> What if thought freed itself from common sense and decided to think only at the extreme point of its singularity? What if it mischievously practiced the bias of paradox, instead of complacently accepting its citizenship in the doxa? What if it thought difference differentially, instead of searching out the common elements underlying difference? (Keenan 1987).

Second, related to this, we might take up his technique of reversal, sometimes as a way of thinking against himself, but also as a form of active critique. In reversal, Foucault's strategy is to take a traditional interpretation of a historical or social event and, as the method suggests, look at it in an opposite direction. He means reversal here in the sense of a subversion or an over-turning, as a means of refuting and inverting assumptions of origin. 'The principle of reversal hence may be seen as a way of *politicizing the de-politicized*, self-warranting accounts of discourse, as way of making discourse visible, and visibly connected to multiple prospective origins and forms of realization' (Hook 2007, pp. 18–19).

Third, his playful but productive tendency to want to use key words in different senses, with different meanings—which is often complicated or compounded by his loose or changing use of key terms at different times in his work, and by the limits and vagaries of translation. All of this sets, what Aimee Howie calls Foucault's 'sharp inconclusiveness', over and against 'the palor of codified theory', that so many commentators strive to impose on him. Thus, in important respects I begin this book with a much clearer sense of what I do not want to write, what I want to avoid, than what I do want to write. I am more concerned with style and practice than with method and argument.

Fourth, his use of illustration or demonstration as a technique of analysis; 'acts of demonstration; by showing rather than saying' (Osborne 2009, p. 126), and this is in part related to the problem of trying to speak to that something 'a little beneath history'. That is, Foucault, sought to _show_ rather than to rehearse a method as such—Osborne (p. 126) suggests that 'style should be *opposed* to method'. Osborne in his paper, also titled *Foucault as Educator*, gives particular attention to Foucault's style in relation to his lectures in particular and draws on Deleuze's comments.

Deleuze says 'Style is a set of variations in language, a modulation, and a straining of one's whole language toward something outside it' (Deleuze 1995, p. 140). (This relates again to limits—of writing and language.)

While Foucault's significance as a social theorist is undisputed, his importance for education and as an educationalist is frequently overlooked. This book considers Foucault as educator in three main ways. First, what his work says about modernist education as a social and political practice (Chap. 1). That is, education as a form of what Allen (2014) calls *benign violence*—which operates through mundane, quotidian disciplinary technologies and expert knowledges to construct a 'pedagogical machine'. Second, an exploration of his 'method' as a form of critique (Chap. 2). That is, critique as a way of showing that things are 'not as necessary as all that', of identifying what is intolerable. What I want to suggest is that critique itself, in Foucault's sense, is education of a kind. Third, a discussion of some of his later work on subjectivity and in particular on 'the care of the self' or what we might call 'a pedagogy of the self' (Chap. 3), drawing on a range of previous attempts, I try to sketch the outlines of what a Foucauldian education might look like. In each chapter I will introduce and discuss some relevant examples from educational settings to illustrate and enact Foucault's analytics. To an extent, Chap. 1 primarily addresses the problem of power, Chap. 2 that of truth, and Chap. 3 subjectivity.

Heuristically at least the first section of the book considers what education looks like in Foucauldian terms as a history of dominations, a history of the docile subject if you like, and that is set over and against in section three what education might look like if we take seriously Foucault's later work on the care of the self and self-formation—a history of the active subject, if you like. Squeezed between these two sections is a different take on Foucault as educator, one offered by Lynn Fendler (2010). She uses pedagogical theory to characterise Foucault's philosophical legacy, and says 'we can classify Foucault's philosophy as being most closely related to modelling, or "teaching by example" (p. 184). Fendler goes on to say: 'By means of provocative devices, Foucault's philosophy facilitates our ability to think critically. By means of poetic devices, Foucault's work also exemplifies for us a particular mode of critical thinking' (p. 184). However, in doing this he seeks to avoid the authority of the teacher. He is not suggesting that we should do as he does or as he says. He is suspicious of imperative philosophy, which as he says 'seems to me to be very flimsy when delivered from a teaching institution' (Foucault 2009, Lecture 1, p. 3). Rather he offers what he calls 'tactical pointers' (p. 3) which may serve to orient us in 'the circle of struggle and truth' (p. 3). This captures nicely the way in which I address Foucault's work of *critique* and his method of study, but it also underpins the approach of the book as a whole.

Now if that seems worthwhile then you might read on and see how things go. If not there is plenty of Foucault to be read in the original. I will try to be provocative and relevant and I will draw on a range of other writers who have taken Foucault seriously. When I cannot do better myself I will quote from their work. However, I cannot write outside of the things I describe. I have been an educational subject of some sort throughout my life, from the time my mother began to teach me to read, to my current endeavours as a professor of sociology of education. I began as a child of welfare state schooling and I am now a neoliberal academic. When I write about the history of education and about its contemporary condition I write about myself. When I look for other ways in which we might be 'educated' I write about my own attempts at some kind of self-formation. Nonetheless, do not worry, the personal will only intrude explicitly into the text on one or two occasions.

I could not have written this book without being able to read and draw on the thinking of a number of other writers who have taken the relevance of Foucault's work to education seriously. I write with, for, among and alongside them—Michael Peters, Roger Deacon, Tina Besley, Ansgar Allen, Lynn Fendler, Bernadette Baker, Maria Tamboukou, James Marshall, Keith Hoskin, Patrick Bailey, Deborah Youdell, Julie Allan, and Mark Olssen among others.

So the book is very much an exploration, a search for possibilities of thought. It contains some false starts and dead ends. And I write not as a philosopher of education but as a sociologist. I am interested in a worldly Foucault, a Foucault of struggles and practices, and of contingencies. I will write about education with a sense of history and of power-relations, with one eye of the contemporary 'context of context' of education—neoliberalism. However, I will not replay the history of education outlined in *Foucault, Power and Education* (Ball 2013), or at least only when absolutely necessary.

So to be clear, the book explores the possibilities of Foucault as Educator in three different ways.

First, after a very brief account of Foucault's own education and his pedagogical practice, I look as some of the ways in which education is depicted in his work— often as asides. This will also involve a consideration of the way in which Foucault's work is deployed in educational research as a dystopia. I will argue that more generally Foucault's anti-humanism, combined with his analysis of institutions makes education impossible—that is *Foucault as uneducator*. In relation to this, I begin to adumbrate a genealogy of pedagogy and look at contemporary education using some Foucauldian tools and techniques to suggest some shifts and continuities between a modern and a neoliberal educational episteme, a shift that is from a politics of education (discipline) to an economics of education (governmentality). Second, what can we learn from Foucault as a philosopher, what sort of practices do his methods offer to us in relation to how we live now? This will involve first some consideration of what he means by *critique*, this requires an aside to his conception of power (getting the right target). Third, as indicated above, I foray hesitantly into a consideration of what some of the later of Foucault's lectures at the College de France (Foucault 2011, 2013), and some of his later books and interviews, might say to or about an education that is not captured within the institutional niceties of modernism or the neoliberal logic of investment. This will in part rest on an attempt to separate out resistance, as a modernist political practice, from refusal, as a neoliberal political practice—the refusal of what we have become.

The text is discontinuous, 'a bit disjointed and scattered' (Foucault 2010b, Lecture 1, p. 2), and it breaks off at points of failure (Foucault 2 lectures on power), in his words it consists of a set of abutments, strings of dots. The book consists of a number of tactical interventions and digressions—attempts to use Foucault's tools and his different bodies of work to think differently about education, education history and education policy—about what it education and latterly about what it might be.

Foucault's Education

Foucault had a privileged education. He had an English nanny and private lessons at home. He attended Lycee Henri-IV in Poitiers from 1936 and initially did well, but in his exams in 1940 he did very badly and had to re-sit some. He was removed from the school by his mother and enrolled in a religious school, the College Saint-Stanislas. During his time there his philosopher teacher was arrested and deported to Germany. A tutor was recruited to teach him philosophy, but was not a success. He passed his *bac* in 1943 and set his sights on studying philosophy at the Ecole Normale Superior which recruited mainly from elite Parisan lycees. He failed in his initial attempt to qualify for entry, he was disappointed but not discouraged. He moved to Paris to attend another Lycee Henri-IV, to prepare better, where he was taught briefly by Jean Hyppolite, whose work he frequently acknowledged as key to his vocation. He attended an interview for entry to ENS in July 1946, Geogres Canguilhem was one of the interviewers, and came fourth in the list of 38 students admitted that year. In a lecture in 1982 he said that in his day education of the child was primarily and apprenticeship in silence.

He did not enjoy life at the ENS 'He was a solitary, unsociable boy, whose relationships with others were very complex and often conflict ridden' (Eribon 1991, p. 25). It was neither a good time nor a good place to be homosexual. He was taught and befriended by Louis Althusser and briefly joined the Communist Party. He took his written exams in 1950 and was ranked 29th, which came as a surprise to him and his teachers and affected him deeply. He retook the very long exams (6–7 hours of writing) and an oral in 1951 and tied for 3rd place, obtaining his *aggregation*—which would qualify him to teach at secondary school and university. He decidedly did not want to be a schoolteacher and instead gained a scholarship to the *Fondation Thiers*, where he spent one year before being appointed as a part-time assistant lecturer at the University of Lille, but he continued to live in Paris and later was given some part-time teaching duties at ENS. In 1956 he moved to be Director of the *Maison de France* in Uppsala, and in 1958 he moved to a similar role in Warsaw. He returned to Paris in 1960 and took up a full-time post at the University of Clermont-Ferrand having completed his doctorate that year. He was more settled and extremely productive but in September 1966 moved to be Professor of Philosophy at the University of Tunis, from where he observed the events of 'May 68'. One of the responses to those events was a set of reforms of Higher Education which included the creation of a new university on the outskirts of Paris—the Vincennes Experimental University Centre. Foucault was appointed to establish and run the philosophy department and he wanted its teaching to address the political analysis of society and the analysis of domains of science.

Among others he recruited Etienne Balibar, Michel Serres and Jacques Ranciere as teachers. Things did not go well, student protests continued, the university descended into chaos. From this experience Foucault emerged as 'the very figure of the militant intellectual' (Eribon 1991, p. 210). The students had taught him as much as he taught them. He left a department that was as vibrant as it was conflicted.

In 1968 College of France Professor Jean Hyppolite died and a replacement had to be found. On 12 April 1970 Foucault was elected as Professor of the History of Systems of Thought. He delivered his inaugural lecture in December 1970. He continued to teach the 12 lecture series required of him by the College de France every year but one until his death. The series became 'one of the events of Parisian intellectual life' (Eribon 1991, p. 222). The lecture theatre was always packed, sometimes 2000 people attended, with standing room only for latecomers. He spoke surrounded by tape recorders. He bemoaned the fact that with such a large group discussion was impossible and 'with no feedback, the lecture turns into a show' (Foucault 1975, p. 9); and Macey maintains (1993, p. 242) that he was always nervous. He spoke quickly and rather monotonously for 2 hours, reading a prepared text. He found the lecture theatre a lonely place (Macey 1993, p. 245) but enjoyed more the related seminars, access to which he restricted. The courses became opportunities for Foucault to try out his ideas for books, to think out loud and reflect, but over time he became increasingly weary of the obligation. Over the years he also gave lecture series at many universities around the world—most of which are now published. He continued to use his lectures as vehicles for developing his programme of research. By all accounts, at the College de France Foucault was a formidable and demanding teacher, although his seminars were more collaborative he could be acerbic and devastating as a critic. He understood the 'power' of the teacher but Deacon (2006, p. 184) suggests that Foucault was 'undoubtedly a little naïve in believing that his lectures at the College de France (where students only attend what they want and when they want), he managed to avoid exercising power over his audience'. His later lectures in the US seem much more relaxed and he made himself accessible to students. His interviews also convey a strong pedagogical tone. There is little we can learn about pedagogy from Foucault the teacher, he worked within the constraints of his role. His teaching always seemed as much about the process of his own thinking and development as it did about engaging with students but often consisted of provocations he hoped would lead others to do work. Teaching was a means through which he could think differently.

References

Allen, A. (2014). *Benign violence: Education in and beyond the age of reason.* Basingstoke: Palgrave Macmillan.

Ball, S. J. (2013). *Foucault, power and education.* London, New York: Routledge.

Deleuze, G. (1995). *Gilles Deleuze's interview on foucault, 'Life as a Work of Art' negotiations: 1972–1990* (M. Joughin, Trans.). (pp. 94–101). New York: Columbia University Press

Eribon, D. (1991). *Michel foucault.* Cambridge, MA: Harvard University Press.

Fendler, L. (2010). *Michel foucault*. London and New York: Bloomsbury.

Foucault, M. (1975). *I, pierre riviere, having slaughtered my Mother, my Sister and my Brother*. Hramondswoth: Penguin.

Foucault, M. (1988). Truth, power, self: An interview with Michel Foucault. In L. H. Martin, H. Gutman & P. Hutton (Eds.), *Technologies of the self: A seminar with Michel Foucault* (pp. 9–15). London: Tavistock.

Foucault, M. (2009). *Security, territory, Population: Lectures at the College de France 1977–78*. New York: Palgrave Macmillan.

Foucault, M. (2010a). *The birth of biopolitics: Lectures at the College de France 1978–1979*. Basingstoke: Palgrave Macmillan.

Foucault, M. (2010b). *The government of the self and others: Lectures at the College de France 1982–1983*. Basingstoke: Palgrave.

Foucault, M. (2011). *The Courage of truth: Lectures at the College de France 1983–84*. London: Palgrave Macmillan.

Foucault, M. (2013). *The will to know: Lectures at the College de France 1983–84*. Basingstoke: Palgrave Macmillan.

Foucault, M. (nd.). Self-writing. Retrieved May 17, 2012 from http://itsy.co.uk/archive/sisn/Pos/green/Foucault.doc.

Foucault, M. (Ed.). (1997). *What is enlightenment*. New York: Semotext(e).

Gutting, G. (Ed.). (1994). *Introduction: Michel foucault: A user's manual*. Cambridge: Cambridge University Press.

Hook, D. (2007). *Foucault, psychology and the analytics of power*. Basingstoke: Palgrave Macmillan.

Keenan, T. (1987). The "paradox" of knowledge and power: Reading foucault on a bias. *Political Theory, 15*(1), 5–37.

Macey, D. (1993). *The lives of michel foucault*. London: Hutchinson.

Osborne, T. (2009). Foucault as educator. In M. A. Peters, A. C. Besley, M. Olssen, S. Maurer & S. Weber (Eds.), *Governmentality studies in education*. Rotterdam: Sense.

Sawicki, J. (1991). *Disciplining foucault: Feminism, power and the body*. New York: Routledge.

Chapter 1
The Impossibility of Education

Abstract This chapter explores education as one nexus of Foucault's three vectors of analysis or 'aspects of experience'—truth, power, and subjectivity. It further considers how the changing emphases between these vectors in Foucault's oeuvre can enable us to think about education differently. I put these vectors to work in relation to a exploratory and very provisional genealogy of pedagogy and the school. Finally, the chapter discusses what such analyses mean in terms of education as a philosophical practice, and suggests, as far as the early and mid period work of Foucault is concerned, in relation to his strident anti-humanism, that education is impossible.

Keywords Truth · Subjectivity · Power · Pedagogy · Anti-humanism

> Education may well be, as of right, the instrument whereby every individual, in a society like our own, can gain access to any kind of discourse. But we well know that in its distribution, in what it permits and in what it prevents, it follows the well-trodden battle-lines of social conflict. Every educational system is a political means of maintaining or of modifying the appropriation of discourse, with the knowledge and the powers it carries with it. (Foucault 1972, p. 227)

> … Foucault's work, including the later work focussed on governmentality, offers hints, fragments and building blocks for a genealogy of pedagogical practice and knowledge. At the core of the enterprise as Foucault conducts it there is, of course, the linkage between investigation and problematisation. What is it that we wish to problematise when we study the genealogy of education? (Gordon 1991, p. 200)

I want to do three things in this chapter. First, to think about education, or perhaps more precisely schooling, as one nexus of Foucault's three vectors of analysis or 'aspects of experience'—truth, power, and subjectivity and their 'messy interactions' (Olssen 2006, p. 185). Second, to consider how the changing emphases between these vectors in Foucault's oeuvre can enable us to think about education differently. Bearing in mind that 'neither are reduced one to the other nor absorbed one by the others, but whose relations are constitutive of one another' (cited in Flynn 2005, p. 262). Taking up some of the 'hints, fragments and building blocks

© The Author(s) 2017
S.J. Ball, *Michel Foucault*, SpringerBriefs on Key Thinkers in Education,
DOI 10.1007/978-3-319-50302-8_1

for a genealogy of pedagogical practice and knowledge' that Gordon notes above, I put these vectors to work in relation to a exploratory and very provisional genealogy of pedagogy and the school (see Chap. 2 for a discussion of genealogy as a method), and use Foucault's tools to re-work or revise Foucault's analysis of the school. That is, I want to say something about pedagogy in relation to truth, the institution of the modern school in relation to power, and the neoliberal school and neoliberal education in relation to subjectivity. I will also give some examples of the way in which the possibilities of these analyses have been taken up in the sociology of education. Third, and briefly, I will consider what such analyses mean in terms of education as a philosophical practice, and suggest, as far as the early and mid period work of Foucault is concerned, in relation to his strident anti-humanism, that education is impossible. Rather what we call education is a complex of power relations concerned with the manufacture and management of individuals and the population—a key space of regulation or biopower. The school is one of those sites where the body and population meet, where normality confronts degeneracy. The population becomes 'a sort of technical-political object of management and government' (Foucault 2009, p. 70).[1]

> The population spans everything from the biological substrate, through species- life, to the graspable surface of the public. From the species to the public; we have here a whole field of new realities, realities in the sense that they are pertinent elements for mechanisms of power, the pertinent space within which and on which one must act. (Ibid p. 75)

Foucault and Education

Deacon (2006) points out that only in two short texts does Foucault 'focus primarily and almost exclusively on education' (p. 178),[2] and that 'to date no text has marshaled together in one place all of Foucault's references to the field' (p. 178). However, he also suggests that Foucault's detailed studies of madness, punishment, sexuality and the human sciences provide concepts, techniques and arguments of very great relevance to educational studies. As Devine-Eller says 'Though Foucault himself never wrote an extended history of education, he could easily have' (Devine-Eller 2004, p. 1).

On the other hand, Hoskin (1990) argues that Foucault was a 'crypto-educationalist and that *learning under examination* is a key element of his analytic'. Hoskin argues that 'What we may well need to consider is how "the educational" may in different epochs, in different ways, function as the hyphen in the power/knowledge relation' (p. 51). Power/knowledge demands, Hoskin asserts, 'a third term' (p. 52) and 'can that third term properly be other than an educational

---

[1]Perhaps, as Patrick Bailey suggested to me, this points up the tension in Foucault's work between his historical narratives of power and the analyses of complexes of power—dispositifs.

[2]In addition Foucault's later work address education in the classical period in a number of ways.

term?'—examination. I take this up to some extent below but in a different way from that intended by Hoskin when I consider the possible difference between the examination and the test as bases for teacher expertise. Allen (2014) makes a similar point to Hoskin when he says 'The cold objective tools of modern examination would seem to epitomize the modern perspective' (p. 15). I am not entirely convinced by that and will try out for size a slightly different and more orthodox argument focused on expertise as the third term between power and knowledge.

The work that contains the most and most direct references to education, or more correctly to the school as an institution is *Discipline and Punish* (Foucault 1979). This book, and its analysis of the modern institution, has generated a huge number of sociological and philosophical papers (e.g. Ball 2001; Besley 2005; Edwards 2002; Evans and Holroyd 2004; Green 1998; Perryman 2006; Peters 2001; Popkewitz 1998). In these terms the school is quintessentially a disciplinary institution which through the organization and division of space and time and the concomitant organisation and division of learners formed a key part of the new urban landscape of late 18th early 19th centuries as a constituent of the urban grid of power. The rhythms, repetitions and cycles of the school produced an 'anatomo-chronological schema' firmly rooted in the modern *episteme*,[3] alongside, drawing from and feeding into the work of prisons, hospitals and factories. Alongside hospitals, prisons, welfare offices and local government, schools literally and in effect constituted the architecture of the modern state, as a 'disposition of space for economico-political ends' (Foucault 1979, p. 148), drawing on existing disciplinary/pastoral/pedagogical practices and new disciplinary knowledges (see below). The school emerged as a regional institution in a more general network of power, as part of the 'geo-politics' of 'the carceral city' (p. 307). Schooling is a perfect example of what Foucault called the 'daemonic' coupling of the 'city game' and the 'shepherd-game' (Gordon 1991, p. 8) with teachers as a 'secular political pastorate'. Thus, Foucault suggests: 'The town posed new and specific economic and political problems of government technique' (Foucault 2009, p. 64) and that in response a 'very complex technology of securities appeared' (p. 64), of which the school became a key element; a particular site in which cleanliness, order and productivity could be addressed.

The methodology of schooling is a materiality of power. On the one hand, the power of bricks and mortar. As Hunter (1996, p. 147) puts it 'it is not educational principles that are central to the role of education systems but school premises'. On the other, there is the materiality of bodies and of social events—and a set of techniques and practices; the diagnosis, the confession, the classroom question, and as noted already, the examination. The body is 'the inscribed surface' of educational events and it 'bears and manifests the effects of regulating discourses' (Foucault 1984, p. 82).

---

[3]An episteme is the system of concepts that defines knowledge for a given intellectual era, the conditions of possibility for knowledge. What Foucault also called the 'intellectual subconscious' of scientific disciplines.

In the late 19th century new technologies of measurement and examination quickly gave rise to a proliferation of 'scholastic accountancy'. As Donald (1992, p. 31) says: 'there was nothing covert or mysterious about these techniques. They were built into the very structure and routine of the schools'. Learners are 'seen' and 'modified' and 'broken down', by age and sometimes by gender, by ability, by 'need', in relation to talents or capabilities or forms of specialty or abnormality. Foucault draws our attention to these mundane processes and quotidian practices, the minute institutional divisions and categorisations and 'the little tactics of habit' (1979, p. 149) that are part of 'an apparatus of total and circulating mistrust' (ibid p. 158). Schooling was built literally on the contradictory bases of uniformity and individuality, a collectivist vision mediated within the methodologies of division and differentiation.

> Take for an example an educational institution: the disposal of its space, the meticulous regulations which govern its internal life, the different activities which are organized there, the diverse persons who live there or meet one another, each with his own functions, his well-defined character-all these things constitute a block of capacity-communication-power. The activity which ensures apprenticeship and the acquisition of aptitudes or types of behavior is developed there by means of a whole ensemble of regulated communications (lessons, questions and answers, orders, exhortations, coded signs of obedience, differentiation marks of the value of each person and of the levels of knowledge) and by the means of a whole series of power processes (enclosure, surveillance, reward and punishment, the pyramidal hierarchy). (Foucault 1982, pp. 218–219)

Indeed, the very idea of the school, its materiality, its imaginary, its articulation within policy and practice came to be centered on and enacted in terms of a machinery of differentiation and classification, and concomitantly of exclusion. Power was literally made visible and visceral as architecture and space, and as practices of division and exclusion.[4] The power of discipline is 'one of analysis' (Foucault 1979, p. 197) to locate and separate, that is 'power organizes an analytic space' (p. 143) a 'cellular space' and a 'therapeutic space' (p. 144), a space of 'precision' (p. 143) and distribution. Here power produces reality as a domain of objects articulated in specific rituals of truth. As highlighted by Hoskin and Allen, Foucault says the school became in the 19th century an 'apparatus of uninterrupted examination' (1979, p. 186), the examination was the main mechanism of simultaneous evaluation and comparison 'woven into [the school] through a constantly repeated ritual of power' (1979, p. 186). While the learner is made visible in all of this power is rendered invisible. The learner sees only the tasks and the tests which they must undertake as a subject in the 'eye of power' (Foucault 1980). This is very different from the 'sovereign' and 'episodic' exercise of power. Here power is an everyday, socialised and embodied phenomenon and this provides the basis of what Michael Gallagher calls 'Orwellian readings of Foucault' (http://socialtheoryapplied.com/2013/04/04/using-foucault-in-school-research-thinking-beyond-the-panopticon/, accessed 27.07.16).

---

[4]It is in relation to the struggles and conflicts around such exclusion that the *political force* of knowledge (Hook 2007). *Foucault, Psychology and the Analytics of Power*. Basingstoke: Palgrave MacMillan. p. 142) comes into view.

Schools via their own 'arbitrary cruelties' were beginning in the late 19th century to assume their intermediary socializing and civilising role between family and work. Government and opportunity, capability and freedom were juxtaposed in the 'positive liberty' of state schooling. The school developed in relation to a *reluctant* but *necessary* state and a set of uneasy relationships between the state, the teacher and the parent as a modern *dispositif* of government. This was set within a distribution and re-distribution of *responsibilities for governing and means and techniques for governing*. In the 19th century, in a whole myriad of ways, the state began to assume *responsibility* for its citizens. Concomitantly, Foucault argued inside the institutions of responsibility, of which the school was one; 'Technical social science began to take form within the context of administration' (Dreyfus and Rabinow 1983, p. 134). That is, a new agent and means of government emerged— the professional expert. Foucault outlined a diabolical interplay between the modern institution and professional knowledge. I will to come back to this shortly.

Government in the 19th century, as the 'political technology of the body' (Foucault 1979, p. 26), was increasingly concerned with the minds and bodies of its populace, and their wellbeing, as an indicator and facilitator of the wellbeing of the nation and its security. Specifically social and education policy was a response to the *urban* problem. However, as Foucault goes on to argue, there is not just one form of power emerging here in relation to the problem of the urban but two. Not just *discipline* but also *regulation*. There are two techniques and two politics involved here and we need to attend to both, and to their relations. Disciplinary power, on the one hand, which focuses on the individual body, concerned with the 'disciplinary technology of individual dressage' (Stoler 1995, p. 82) and regulatory power, on the other hand, which is concerned with the life of the body of the species, and is 'globalizing' rather than individualizing. This latter is the 'bio-regulation of the state', and is concerned with the internal dangers to society at large (Stoler 1995, p. 82). Much of the sociological work that 'uses' Foucault in relation to the analysis of schooling attends to the former and neglects the latter (see Ball 2013).

Indeed, education policy is a very good example of Foucault's point that 'Population comes to appear above all else to be the ultimate end of government' (Gordon 1991, p. 100) as a resource (see Chap. 2). The population as a resource is garnered and nurtured within 'the mundane objectives of the administrative state— social order, economic prosperity, social welfare' (Hunter 1996, p. 153). This was a new type of political rationality and practice which 'no longer sought to achieve the good life nor merely to aid the prince, but to increase the scope of power for its own sake by bringing the bodies of the state's subjects under tighter discipline' (Dreyfus and Rabinow 1983, p. 137)—making them 'sober, healthy and competitive' (Jones 1990, p. 68). The population comes to be 'considered as a set of processes to be managed at the level and on the basis of what is natural ...' (ibid p. 70). The population becomes 'a sort of technical-political object of management and government' (ibid p. 70). In the 4th lecture in the series *Security, Territory, Population*, Foucault named this new form of government 'governmentality', what he calls a 'singular generality',[5] and begins to refer to 'the governmentalization' of the state' (Foucault 2009, p. 109) which, he goes on to say, ensures the survival of and defines the limits of the state.[6] We thus have the series: 'security—population—government' (p. 88), as opposed to, say, 'discipline—subjects—territorial sovereignty'.

This new series was played out in a whole variety of sites of regulation. 'The watchword now became National Efficiency, a programme for redefining and extending the powers of the state through reforms in government, industry and social organization, as well as education' (Donald 1992, p. 27). This is a shift, as Foucault referred to it, from *territory* to *security* and he looked at scarcity (the movement of goods), town planning, the management of epidemics, as examples of the sorts problems and responses to them that formed the modern state in relation to population, and he considers in particular the role of statistics in mediating and facilitating the relations of state and population, which are articulated in a set of 'new notions' in their field of application—that is, 'case, risk, danger and crisis' (2009, p. 61). He goes on to say that these are all linked to the phenomenon of the town itself' (p. 63). As Rose (1999, p. 232) puts it:

> In analyses of democracy, a focus on numbers is instructive, for it helps us turn our eyes from the grand texts of philosophy to the mundane practices of pedagogy, of counting, of information and polling, and to the mundane knowledges of "grey sciences" that support them.

Foucault suggests that 'there is one element that will circulate between the disciplinary and the regulatory' and which will 'make it possible to control both the disciplinary order of the body and the aleatory events that occur in the biological multiplicity' (2004, p. 253)—that is the norm. This intersection produces what he called 'a normalizing society' within which 'power took possession of life' (p. 253).

---

[5]This 4th lecture was published separately (Green 1998). Born-Again Teaching? Governmentality, "Grammar" and Public Schooling. In T.S. Popkewitz & M. Brennan (Eds.), *Foucault's Challenge: Discourse, Kowledge and Power in Education*. New York: Teachers College Press. Its take-up gave impetus to what is sometimes called '*governmentality studies*' which is one of the most widespread and productive fields in which Foucault's work has been taken forward.

[6]At the end of this fourth lecture Foucault adds a coda which links this new form of analysis back to the work he undertook in *The Order of Things* on the emergence of the modern human sciences —biology, economics and linguistics. He suggests that 'a constant interplay between techniques of power and their object gradually carves out in reality, as a field of reality, population and its specific phenomena. A whole series of objects were made visible for possible forms of knowledge …' (1970, p. 79). Specifically, the possibilities for knowledges of man; the human subject is a 19th Century production for it is then 'that human forces confront purely finitary forces—life, production, language—in such a way that the resulting composite is a form of Man' (Deleuze 1995, p. 99). Here is another point of intersection between archaeology and genealogy. In *Security, Territory and Population*—where Foucault suggests a recontextualisation of the core themes of *The Order of Things* and indeed also revisits, in an unusually direct way, part of the agenda of his 1970 inaugural lecture, *The Order of Discourse*, Foucault rapidly outlines a view of how the changing regimes of knowledge of life, labour and language respectively entered into, and became stakes in historico-political debates and struggles over race, class and nation.

Central to processes of classification Foucault argues, and in a specific relation to statistics (e.g. the bell curve) is *normalisation,* 'the primary and fundamental character of the norm' (1979, p. 57), as a standard that unifies practice. The norm is the point of concatenation—'normalization becomes one of the great instruments of power at the end of the classical age' (1979, p. 184). Power here is the subtle and meticulous control of bodies rather than the deployment of ethical or judicial judgements. This is the point at which anatomo-politics and biopolitics are artic-ulated (Foucault 1980, p. 139). 'The norm is what can be applied to both the body that desires discipline, as well as to the population that desires regularization' (Foucault 2004, p. 262).

These themes and representations of *modern* education remain as pertinent now as they did in the 19th century. The school as a panopticon (Gallagher 2010), the school as surveillance (Hope 2015), the school as a machinery of classifications (Scheer 2011). That is all well and good, and in many ways a very convincing and an eminently 'useful' critique of the institution of the school as a vehicle of gov-ernment, but is it subtle enough? The school and the hospital and the prison maybe equivalent as sites of government, but are they isomorphic? Can we 'usefully' introduce some nuances into the analysis of the modern school? As Gutting sug-gests Foucault's 'analyses are effective precisely because they are specific to the particular terrain of the discipline he is challenging' (1994, p. 3). Perhaps after all it is dangerous to think about schools simply as though they were prisons.

Here I want to both use and trouble Foucault's analysis, and in particular the way it has been taken up by sociologists, to sketch out a somewhat different genealogy of the school; one that explores the articulation of power/knowledge in a different way, in a specific relation to pedagogy and the teacher; and one that unpacks the hyphen (power/knowledge) in relation to the teacher and the teacher's expertise.

Liberal governing, according to Rose, depends on the State's authorization of expert technologies (like the examination—in its various meanings) as forms of authority and these play a key role in the alignment of the political aims of the State with the strategies of experts, as well as the linking of the 'calculations of authorities with the aspirations of free citizens' (Rose 1999, pp. 48–49). Indeed, Rose and Miller (1992, p. 173) assert that 'modern political rationalities and governmental technologies are shown to be linked (my emphasis) to developments in knowledge and to the powers of expertise'. The knowledges, technologies and training provided by the human sciences for the formation of state professionals construct a relationship of management (discipline and regulation) between pro-fessionalism and population. 'The emergence of social science cannot, as you see, be isolated from the rise of this new political rationality, and from this new political technology' (Martin et al. 1988, p. 162). That is to say, teachers, social workers, sanitary engineers, doctors were certificated as state actors and enactors of the state, bringing the gaze of the state to bear upon individual bodies and the population as a whole.

What I offer here is a tactical analysis—an 'imperfect sketch' (Foucault 1972, p. 15)—starting from the problem of the teacher as a state professional in order to open insights into our educational present. That is, I will explore different modes of pedagogy, as different ways in which we are made subject by and subject to education. This will involve addressing a fundamental and debilitating paradox of contemporary educational practice, the basis of which is to some extent already in place. Sharp and Green (1975), Bernstein (1996) and Foucault (1979) himself have all suggested that 'new' or *progressive* educational forms contain the possibility of a more effective 'conduct of conduct' than prior *disciplinary* techniques of pedagogy, through the production of a self managing learner who is attached to the goals of education not through 'methods of correct training' but through forms of freedom —choice and self-determination in the classroom. In effect, these progressive methods both open up more of the learner to the pedagogic gaze and encourage the learner to take greater responsibility for their own 'progress' and improvement—to manage themselves and their learning. This is signaled, for instance, in the most recent reiteration of power/knowledge as pedagogy, that is the discursive shift in policy and expert knowledges from an emphasis on teaching to a focus on learning. Barr and Tagg (1995) offer one rendition of this shift, and adumbrate its entanglement with the *neoliberalisation* of education. A UNESCO document *A Shift from Teaching to Learning* (http://portal.unesco.org/education/en/ev.php-URL_ID= 26923&URL_DO=DO_TOPIC&URL_SECTION=201.html, accessed 27.07.16) indicates something of what is at stake for teachers and for students in this shift.

> Shifting the emphasis from teaching to learning can create a more interactive and engaging learning environment for teachers and learners. This new environment also involves a change in the roles of both teachers and students ... the role of the teacher will change from knowledge transmitter to that of learning facilitator, knowledge guide, knowledge navigator and co-learner with the student. The new role does not diminish the importance of the teacher but requires new knowledge and skills. Students will have greater responsibility for their own learning in this environment as they seek out, find, synthesize, and share their knowledge with others.

Pedagogy, Truth and Expertise

As already noted, Foucault's most extended discussion of education is in the famous third section, 'Discipline', of *Discipline and Punish*. Some of the illustrative material in this section is drawn from one of the most influential French schooling manuals of the early modern period, De La Salle's *Conduite des Écoles Chrétiennes*. Foucault seeks to establish the distinctive features of the pedagogical techniques outlined, as the methods shared with other kinds of institutions; thus, as quoted above he asks: 'Is it surprising that prisons resemble factories, schools, barracks, and hospitals, which themselves all resemble prisons?' Nonetheless, his account of the idea of an educational 'programme' is not straightforward and also has elements drawn from religious institutions and relationships and long established traditions of moral and ascetic training.

> The theme of a perfection towards which the exemplary master guides the pupil became with them that of an authoritarian perfection of the pupils by the teacher; the increasingly rigorous exercises that the ascetic life proposed became tasks of increasing complexity that marked the gradual acquisition of knowledge and good behaviour; the striving of the whole community towards salvation became the collective, permanent competition of individuals being classified in relation to one another. (Foucault 1979, pp. 161–2)

Perhaps we need to think about this in relation to another of Foucault's genealogies. In *Security, Territory, Population* we might read this example slightly differently. It seems to be that this is not a very clear cut case of the new forms of power and of the institution that Foucault seeks to adumbrate in *Discipline and Punish*, rather what we see here is a reiteration of older forms of pastoral power or perhaps a point of transition between to two. Indeed, he says 'Importantly, despite the many strategic reversals and contestations over this form of power, the history of the pastorate as a technology of power is a history from which Western modernity, despite its secular pretensions, has by no means emerged' (2009, p. 165). That is, a 'secular theology'. In *Security, Territory, Population* Foucault undertakes 'an analysis and a bringing to light of the theological grounds of modern practices of power and political subjectivity' (Golder 2009, 157–75). Hunter (1996) makes this very clear in his discussion of what he terms 'spiritual discipline' and he makes two very important points. First, that the school is 'an improvised historical institution—assembled from the moral and material grab-bag of Western culture' (p. 148). Second, that '"critical" educational theory and history has sought to efface the "statist" and Christian lineages of the modern school system' (p. 162). Certainly most of the recent sociological applications of Foucault's analysis of disciplinary technologies to the school have written out 'the pastoral'.

There is also the difficulty here that *Discipline and Punish* and *Security, Territory, Population* mark a point of transition in Foucault's work, a shift in his conceptualisation of power, both its genealogy and its practice, which offer slightly different possible readings of the emergence and the methods of the 19th century state. While *Discipline and Punish* focuses on institutions and disciplinary power, *Security, Territory, Population* focuses on population, *governmentality* and a genealogy of pastoral power. The pastorate he asserts is 'one of the decisive moments in the history of power in Western societies' (p. 185) and argues elsewhere: 'we can see the state as a modern matrix of individualization, or a new form of pastoral power' (Foucault 1982, p. 111). That is to say, while Foucault is relatively clear that while the Christian pastorate forms both the 'background' (p. 165) and the 'prelude' (p. 184) to more recognizably modern forms of government, and that these latter formations 'arise on the basis' of it (p. 193), he is nevertheless not describing a 'massive, comprehensive transfer of pastoral functions from Church to state' (p. 229). In all of this, the technical expertise of the pastor remains somewhat elusive. Pastoral practice is articulated not on the basis of esoteric knowledge but as Foucault observes, '[t]he pastor must really take charge of and observe daily life in order to form a never-ending knowledge of the behavior and conduct of the members of the flock he supervises' (p. 181). The pastor's concern is with the 'spiritual direction' [*direction de conscience*] of the thoughts of his flock—a set of practices that generate 'a truth which binds one to the person who directs one's conscience' (p. 183). The relation of all of this to something we might call pedagogy is unclear.

Nonetheless, by starting with pastoral power, rather than with discipline, we might be able to think about pedagogy as a human science, not with the historical sweep of Foucault's *The Order of Things* (1970) but more specifically focussed on 'the threshold of modernity that we have not yet left behind'—that is focused on the modern school. There will not be space here to address what Foucault (p. x) calls the pedagogical 'calendar of saints and heroes' (like those referred to in *Discipline and Punish*) who contributed to the emergence of 'methods of teaching', and rather I want to place pedagogy in some kind of relation to those Human Sciences that Foucault addresses in *The Order of Things*[7]—economics, linguistics and biology. As Foucault might put it I am only seeking to 'open up' this question as a site for further work.[8]

With some latitude it maybe possible to argue that pedagogy does earn its place in the modern dispositif, alongside the other human sciences, 'as what might have been said at the same time' (that is as having an epistemic resemblance), and in relation to the analysis Foucault lays out in the above. That is to say, in relation to population as a political problem and as the 'subject-object' fundamental to the emergence of economics, linguistics and biology—and quite clearly also pedagogy. Might we also glimpse some commonalities in the 'rules of formation' and 'systems of regulatories' which extend across the 'representations' of economics, linguistics and biology and include pedagogy in the 19th century? That is, we can extend the field of investigation of the human sciences to include 'man in so far as he lives, speaks and produces' (1970, p. 351) and learns. Indeed, Foucault himself raises this possibility in *Discipline and Punish* when he says: 'The school became the place for elaboration for pedagogy … the age of the "examining school" marks the beginnings of a pedagogy that functions as a science' (Foucault 1979, p. 187). Pedagogy, that is, despite its 'invincible impression of haziness, inexactitude and imprecision' (1970, p. 355) produces a space in which that 'strange figure of knowledge' (p. xxiv)—the learner, appears.

As Foucault suggests, the human sciences enabled modern power to circulate through finer channels. They colonised and operated within the institutions of modern power in particular ways. Through their knowledges and technologies, and in and through those institutions, in this case the school and the teacher, they made certain forms of practice possible, indeed necessary. They structured ways of knowing and exercising power that brought into existence esoteric regimes of

---

[7]In *The Order of Things*, Foucault is concerned primarily with three disciplines that emerged in the nineteenth century: philology, biology, and economics.

[8]I do recognise that pedagogy fails many of the 'tests' of coherence that Foucault suggests for what might be considered a human science. He was interested in disciplines on the 'threshold of scientificity' (1972, pp. 186–89), a threshold that pedagogy may never have crossed.

power/knowledge. We can recognize many of these technologies and knowledges still at work in the contemporary school, as evidence of their effectiveness and continuing anonymous necessity. They are embedded in a broader complex of discourses and practices through which childhood and the pupil are 'made up', and normalized, what MacNaughton (2005, p. 30) calls 'officially sanctioned developmental truths of the child'.

However, there is also a problem here, or rather two problems; one with regard to the extent to which the school is simply a modern institution, as noted above, and relatedly the extent of the transition that state education represented from what had existed previously; and one with regard to the extent to which the teacher was able, and is able, to make claims to expertise and instead perhaps remains teetering insecurely on 'the edges of the rift' (1970, p. 250) that 'isolates for us the beginning of a modern manner of knowing empiricities' (p. 250). In other words, it may be that teaching remains caught in the 'impossibility' of knowledge, played out in the 18th century, which is both representative and quasi-transcendental but not *modern*.

So to address these problems I want to erect a ramshackle and tentative periodization of pedagogical knowledge and practice—in an unstable relation to Foucault's own epistemic periodization and his shifting analysis of power/knowledge. I will call these pedagogical periods *early and late modern, progressive and neoliberal*. The first two and the last, in different but related ways, are very clearly focused on economic and political necessities. Progressive pedagogies, exist in a kind of interregnum, as partly subjugated knowledges which when operational articulate the teacher and the teacher's expertise and relation to knowledge in a different way to the others, but also although less clearly, in relation to changing political and economic necessities. Progressivism also, concomitantly, rests on and is realised within relations of power in the classroom but in ways different from the 'pedagogies' that preceded it—indeed this may be an intensification of power. This heuristic periodization also highlights the point noted above about 'reversal and returns' in the genealogy of power. Dean (2010, p. 57) makes the point that genealogy is not just about variation and discontinuity to also 'to show that the past is not so different from today in certain respects'. I am not intending to signal sharp breaks or ruptures, but rather messy and uneven shifts in emphasis and changing combinations of possibility. There is overtime an accumulation, concatenation and interplay of techniques and modes of power within the classroom. So, for example, spectacular public punishments, exercised directly on 'the body of the condemned' remained commonplace in schools until the 1960s, wherein bad behaviour was subject to reparation rather than 'understood'. As Bailey (2015) explains:

> the histories of policy, power and governmentality, taken both separately and together, are ones of multiple lines of descent, of overlap, transformation, transposition, and sometimes even reversals and returns. There is an 'acetate effect' to power and government—material and epistemological remnants and relics of previous regimes may remain rather than disappearing in the shifts from one singularity to another, and power is a heterogeneous phenomenon.

My concern here then is with *what might be* a science of teaching, and the role of esoteric knowledge in relation to pedagogy. That is, pedagogical knowledges as ways of knowing and representing the learner. Concomitantly, the first demarcation (between early and late modern) rests on a fine distinction between the 'examination' and the 'test', between representation and signification, between enumeration and mathematization, between seriation and capacity, and between discipline and regulation, between anatomo and bio.

The examination is one way of representing the child, 'the pinning down of each individual in his own particularity' (1979, p. 192)[9] and as the 'constant exchanger of knowledge; it guaranteed the movement of knowledge from teacher to the pupil' (p. 187) but while the examination is about what the pupil *knows*; 'the test' (as I am using the term here) is the attempt to know what the pupil *is*. As Foucault says the examination is an 'economy of visibility' (Foucault 1979, p. 187) a form of 'compulsory visibility'—very much focused in his account on the *seriation* of activities and characterising of individuals, rather than, in practice, attempts to discover their 'ultimate capacity' (p. 160). The examination is a technique of 'fixing' (p. 189), of transcription, while, I suggest, the test seeks to access 'development' and capacity and to some extent uniqueness. The examination marks, while the test explains. The examination ranks, while the test identifies a distribution in relation to the norm. In some ways here we see the overlay of classical (or indeed very ancient) and modern forms of representation, which continues in our contemporary education—as a 'field of knowledge that is not yet definitively established' (1970, p. 240). While the examination has its basis in 'displayed descriptability' (1970, p. 237)—(see 1979, p. 190), the test suggests and produces 'a certain internal architecture' (1970, p. 237) that is 'outside representation, beyond its immediate visibility, in a sort of behind-the-scenes world even deeper and more dense than representation itself' (p. 239)—that is *intelligence*, or at 'the very heart of things'—genetics. This involves, as Foucault puts it, an escape 'from the space of the table' (p. 239) to an 'internal space' that shatters 'the space of order … the grid of identities and differences' (p. 239). While, it is Foucault's argument that the examination assures 'continuous genetic accumulation … and thereby the fabrication of cellular, organic, genetic and combinatory individuality' (1979, p. 192), this might be a better description of the test.

Perhaps also we can think about this in terms of attempts to 'mathematicize' (1970, p. 245) the understanding of intelligence, in its relation to distribution across the population, over and against the a posteriori empirical sciences 'which employ the deductive forms only in fragments and in strictly localized regions' (p. 246)—like classroom practices. Here there is a tension between psychology or eugenics and pedagogy. Here is the unstable basis of the teacher as professional, in the

---

[9]He goes on to say 'in contrast with the ceremony in which status, birth privilege, function are manifested with all the spectacle of their marks', and yet the history of the sociological analysis of schooling rests exactly on the continuation of the play of privilege in relation to judgement and achievement.

absence of well-grounded claims to expertise. The gaze of the examination is relatively superficial, whereas the test aims to reveal something profound about the learner, their nature and their capabilities. The examination produces 'the collective, permanent, competition of individuals being classified in relation to one another' (1979, p. 162); it is the test that introduces the 'penalty the norm' (p. 183). In a way Foucault conflates the examination with the test and in making schools like prisons and prisons like schools gives primary emphasis to power rather than to power/knowledge, at least in its broader sense.

While it was argued that 'The pedagogic object of elementary education was to understand the nature of children and then develop their faculties to their fullest potential' (Tate 1857 cited in Larsen 2011) in practice schoolteachers were selected and trained as 'ethical exemplars', of a kind. They were trained to be 'virtuous' rather than 'over-educated' (Jones 1990, p. 62). They were discursively positioned as both 'modern' and 'moral' (Larsen 2011), as bastions against chaos and social disorder. They would bring the children of the urban masses under their 'moral observation' (Donald 1992). As with the asylum, the schools sought 'to impose, in a universal form, a morality that will prevail from within upon those who were strangers to it' (Foucault 2001, p. 246). This is what Jones (1990, p. 66) calls a 'technology of morality' or 'scientific morality' based in a form of teacher training in which 'the inculcation of techniques of self-regulation far outweighed the teacher's intellectual training' (p 62). Indeed, rather than an expert the 19th century teacher is both qualified and selected primarily in terms of their moral probity, as father and Judge (Foucault 2001, p. 259), as pastor rather than pedagogue. Rather than their capability to understand the learner they were expected to guide the conduct and the spirit of the child. In *Madness and Civilization* (2001), Foucault makes a similar point about the 18th century asylum (pp. 258–60). Indeed, this early modern pedagogy may have parallel's with Tuke's 'moral therapy'—Foucault argues that the "moral" asylum is 'not a free realm of observation, diagnosis, and therapeutics; it is a juridical space where one is accused, judged, and condemned'. Moral treatment was an approach to mental disorder based on humane psychosocial care or moral discipline that emerged in the 18th century and came to the fore for much of the 19th century, deriving partly from psychiatry or psychology and partly from religious or moral concerns. The anguish of bourgeois morality 'substituted for the free terror of madness the stifling anguish of responsibility' (Foucault 2006a, p. 582).

Pedagogy remained in the 19th century, and even perhaps today, locked in some version of what Foucault calls a 'double affirmation—alternating or simultaneous— of being able and not being able to formalize the empirical' (1970, p. 246)—despite various attempts of different kinds, at different points in time, to establish some basis for formalisation and its location in 'the norms of positivism' (2001, p. 260). Articulated within the 'fracturing' of forms of representation in the 19th century, the teacher is not constituted by expertise, by esoteric bodies of knowledge, but almost entirely by practices, methods of conduct and by their moral responsibilities. The teacher's practice fails to become obscure (2001, p. 261); no clear 'pedagogical

personage' (2001, p. 263) emerges.[10] There is no science of pedagogy within which
the professionalism of the teacher is embedded and legitimated, rather the claims of
teacher 'expertise', in the 19th century and now, are based on two forms of practice;
one of experience and moral probity and the other of performance and outcome
measurement. In the 19th century (as payment by results) and again in the contemporary period (as performance related pay) both are reductive and
de-professionalising. Indeed, for teacher and learner, this is a reversion to 'the table'
as 'the ground for all possible orders, the matrix of all relations, the form in
accordance with which all beings are distributed in their singular individuality'
(1970, p. 251). Both teacher and learner are represented within this visible order,
the taxinomia of the classroom. Here there is no depth, no mystery 'blurred and
darkened by its obscurity' (1970, p. 251) but a simple relation between outcomes
and observation, the surface visibility of practice, made apparent in 'observations',
learning walks, and inspections—this is all about the visible and what can be
recorded as 'the effect of a patterning process—a mere classifying boundary' (1970,
p. 268) between the unsatisfactory and the outstanding, in the criteria for a 'good'
lesson, in four parts or seven. The school in this sense is 'a homogenous space of
orderable identities and differences' (1970, p. 268).

Performance measurement holds its subjects 'in a mechanism of objectification'
(1970, p. 187), a ceremony of power 'manifest only by its gaze' (p. 188). Again, in
passing Foucault seems to note a point of difference between the examination which
'has remained extremely close to the disciplinary power that shaped it' (p. 226)
and its:

> ... speculative purification by integrating itself with such sciences as psychology and
> psychiatry. And, in effect its appearance in the form of tests, interviews, interrogations and
> consultations is apparently in order to rectify the mechanisms of discipline; educational
> psychology is supposed to correct the rigours of the school... (Ibid p. 226)

In a sense, if we think about education and the school archeologically that may
suggest something different from if we think about the school genealogically. In
Discipline and Punish (1979, p. 191), Foucault asks the question whether 'procedures of writing and registration' the 'mechanisms of examination' and this 'new
type of power over bodies', is 'the birth of the sciences of man', and yet in some
ways, he fails to unpick the differences within the epistemology of the modern
institution between fixity and *developmentalism*, and, in the school at least, the
continuing interplay between status and calculation. That is, we may explore some
possibilities for analysis in the gaps between some aspects of archaeology and some
aspects of genealogy, between *The Order of Things* and *Discipline and Punish*. The
point is not to find fault with Foucault but to use him by exploring a mismatch
between the epistemic/archaeological analysis of the human sciences in *The Order
of Things* and the genealogy of power in *Discipline and Punish*.

---

[10]The celebrations of great teachers remain rooted in personality and morality, in belief and trust
and expectations rather than in science.

What I am suggesting is that we might think about the school in the 19th century not as the epitome of modernism but as a site of tensions between the classical and modern episteme.[11] For Foucault the modern institution 'required the involvement of definite relations of knowledge in relations of power; it called for a technique of over-lapping subjection and objectification' (1979, p. 305). That was not the case in the early modern school. Almost all sociological analysis that seeks to employ Foucault to interrogate the schools lean heavily on power rather than on power/knowledge [e.g. Power Relations in Pedagogy (Gore 1997)] in part at least this is the result of the absence of classroom techniques which rely upon objectification and intelligibility and the predominance of 'means of correct training', that is the absence of pedagogy as a human science.

Late Modern Pedagogy—Is no Pedagogy at All

Perhaps then we need to look elsewhere, other than to *discipline*, to grasp that which is *modern* about education. Following Foucault, a science of education begins to emerge within a different vector of power—that is *regulation* or biopower, the management of life itself, focused on the problem of population. This science sits at the intersection of reproduction and opportunity, the Janus face of educational politics. This is articulated within what Allen (2014) calls *meritocracies*— and 'a connection between eugenic rationality and the pursuit of economic health' (p. 145), indeed 'an alignment between modes of power that defined interwar eugenic history'. I have discussed this as a 'history of blood' (Ball 2013) and Allen explores the complex relations in education between eugenics, economic efficiency and social mobility. He also contests Rose's attempt to confine the specificity of eugenics to the first half of the 20th century (pp. 134–35)—I will come back to that. From these relations emerges what Jones (1990) calls 'the bio-teacher', and he goes on to note that:

> In teacher-training courses inspected by the Board of Education after 1902, the syllabi in 'Principles of teaching' demonstrate a growing concern with the psychology of child development, hygiene, physical training, and housecraft. The teacher accordingly acted alongside the medical officer in 'detecting and dealing with physically and mentally defective children' and devising 'methods of teaching hygiene to children' (syllabus for the Boards 1905–14). (p. 73)

My concern is not to rehearse the history of eugenics but to make the point that it is at this point, focused on 'intelligence' and 'the test', that we see the initial traces of the modernity that Foucault sketches out in *The Order of Things*. It is here, in the practices of testing and statistics, in the 'laboratory' rather than the classroom, that we see the attempt to produce a science of education, in the esoteric knowledge of child

---

[11]Henriques, Hollway et al. (2005, pp. 166–168) outline some aspects of shifts from a monitorial to what I have called an early modern pedagogy (pp. 166–168).

psychology, rather than in the quoditian techniques of examination. The 'methods' of eugenics act back on the classroom to construct certain possibilities of pedagogy and organization but in relation to a more general strategy of biopower—'distributing the living in the domain of value and utility' (Foucault 1981, p. 144). As Foucault argues, the modern state exercises its power, and governs, 'through the administration of life; it is preoccupied with life itself, rather than death' (Foucault 2009, cited in Ball 2013, p. 59). The role of eugenic psychology in the re-working of forms of state power is noted by Allen.

> Cattell hoped that the scientific expert would replace an erstwhile pastorate in guiding us towards the social good. As he put it, 'society must have an adequate supply of watchers in the field of sociological and psychological research in order that the consequences of modified moral laws may be accurately worked out'. (Allen 2014, p. 144)

It is here at the beginning of the 20th century that our phenomenological horizon is ruptured, opening up 'man' as an object of study, a focus for 'objective' scientific research. It is in this way that we begin to see ourselves and others as objects, as part of a new and contingent modality of being of western man.[12]

Even here we might raise doubts about how far eugenics had escaped from the classical form of knowledge and remained locked into an 'old fixism' (Foucault 1970, p. 274) and 'the image of the continuous scale' (p. 272), clinging 'passionately to the immobility of things' (p. 274). It might be said that there is a failure to engage with 'life itself' and to recognise the 'discontinuity of livings forms' (p. 275). The history of life itself—evolution—was transformed into a history of lives by developmental psychology rather than eugenics, and crucially in the former life was conceived in relation to 'to the conditions of existence' (p. 274)—the conditions of educability (see for example Floud and Halsey 1961). Henriques et al. (2005, p. 170) make this point, tracing the beginnings of the 'child study movement' to Darwin's study of his own son—*A Biographical Sketch of an Infant* (1840, 1887). Perhaps taking the parallels with Foucault's discussion of biology too far, it might be said that while eugenics 'affirms, with the limits of the individual, the exigencies of his life', developmentalism marks beneath 'the murmuring of death' (1970, p. 279).

'The test' and 'intelligence' clearly have a relationship to the 'examination', at least in mid 20th century England[13] but the latter is, I suggest rooted in older pre-modern technologies, in teasing out a distinction between them, we can think about the ways in which pedagogy and psychology sit together both uneasily and seamlessly. Together they assure that regulation and discipline cover 'the whole surface that lies between the organic and the biological' (Foucault 2004, p. 253). But crucially, Foucault argues that 'the one element that will circulate between the disciplinary and the population alike' (p. 252) is the norm and all its statistical paraphernalia. In particular, the 'normal curve had within it deep assumptions of

---

[12]This is as Foucault argues, the duality of man—as both an object in the world, an object of study, and an experiencing subject through which the world is constituted.

[13]11+ Norwood etc.

unity by which individuals could be compared on the same conceptual space to the entire population', a 'regime of truth' from which 'it has been almost impossible for any individual to escape' (Olssen 1993, p. 165).

This late modern pedagogy involves a move from 'reading' the child as a surface, to a depth psychology whereby the child is measured and known through the techniques of testing—uncovering the truth of the child. We find *ability or intelligence*, as an effect or articulation of the norm, produced at the heart of schooling, the very point at which teaching could articulate a form of knowledge which related pedagogy to population, and classroom practice to a general theory of management, distribution and entitlement. However, child psychology itself was also subject to change—a move from determinism to developmentalism. As Henriques et al. (2005, p. 4) put it:

> … on the one side of the battle-field of psychology stood the forces of administrative regulation, grinding out the norms: IQ scores; taxonomies of skills; personality inventories; assessment of potential and motivation. On the other side stood the heroes of individual development and the brigades of free expression: spontaneity; self-expression; satisfaction.

Olssen (2006) outlines the similarities and differences between these two psychologies of individual differences. They are he says, 'both founded on biologism and an individualist bias' (p. 176); that is, set within and playing out the 'idea of possessive individualism' (p. 180) which has 'become axiomatic to liberal democratic thought (p. 180). But he contrasts the biological determinism of eugenics with cognitive development psychologies that 'accorded biology a less direct role but still conceptualised the individual as a unitary rational actor' (p. 181). The relationship to the teacher, and the teacher and pedagogy are constructed differently in each case.

Progressive Pedagogy (Bernstein 1990, p. 72)

I want to argue that the shift from measurement to developmentalism addresses an intensification of power which is more focused on the question of who we are and who we might become than our performances. That is, a new 'heterogeneous and indistinct' (Dean 2007, p. 91) form of power. As Nealon (2008) points out there are two possible readings of Foucault's later work, as either abandonment of power or its intensification, both readings are right (see Chap. 3).

There is an immediate and serious problem here. That is, the limits of space in relation to the complexity, history and heterogeneity of what might be understood as progressive pedagogy. All that is possible here is to gesture towards some of the distinctions—in terms of power, knowledge and subjectivity—between what I have called modern and progressive pedagogies. Most pertinently here, there is the relation of pedagogy to knowledge (esoteric knowledge on the one hand and knowledge of the child on the other, and their relation) and the fabrication of the teacher as some sort of expert, as a pedagogue.

Crudely I am suggesting here that we glimpse a version of the teacher as expert, a teacher who is able to deploy theoretically informed practice in the classroom. I will outline this in part by drawing upon Basil Bernstein, whose discussions of what he calls *invisible pedagogies*, have some kind of affinity with some aspects of Foucault's work on governmentality; and less directly on Henriques et al.'s (2005) seminal analysis of child-centred pedagogy and its relationships with developmental psychology. Their focus is primarily on the learner I want to think more about how this pedagogical move constituted and made historically possible a new kind of teacher—a pedagogue. To be clear, I am not referring here to the classical tradition of progressivism (see Larabee 2005)[14] but rather a rough amalgam of some principles of progressivism with some of the insights of developmental psychology that were distilled into the preparation of teachers in the post-war Teacher Training College. This was never a coherent and unified body of knowledge, but drew loosely on the sociology, philosophy and psychology of education to construct a classroom imaginary superficially very different from the machinery of 19th century schooling. This was an imaginary and a set of practices and practical classroom arrangements that received in England a fragile and temporary state legitimation in the *Plowden Report* (1967).[15] The Report presented arguments for a new kind of schooling directly related to claims to the esoteric knowledge of child development.

> 9. At the heart of the educational process lies the child. No advances in policy, no acquisitions of new equipment have their desired effect unless they are in harmony with the nature of the child, unless they are fundamentally acceptable to him. We know a little about what happens to the child who is deprived of the stimuli of pictures, books and spoken words; we know much less about what happens to a child who is exposed to stimuli which are perceptually, intellectually or emotionally inappropriate to his age, his state of development, or the sort of individual he is. We are still far from knowing how best to identify in an individual child the first flicker of a new intellectual or emotional awareness, the first readiness to embrace new sets of concepts or to enter into new relations.

> 10. Knowledge of the manner in which children develop, therefore, is of prime importance, both in avoiding educationally harmful practices and in introducing effective ones. In the last 50 years much work has been done on the physical, emotional and intellectual growth of children. There is a vast array of facts, and a number of general principles have been established.

As David Gillard explains the context in which the report was written and read:

> The context in which the Committee worked was characterised by an increasingly liberal view of education and society. 'Plowden's membership and terms of reference were a product of the optimism and belief in social engineering of its time' (Kogan 1987).

---

[14]**Progressive education** is a pedagogical movement that began in the late nineteenth century; it has persisted in various forms to the present. Progressive education can be traced back to the works of John Locke and Jean-Jacques Rousseau, both of whom are known as forerunners of ideas that would be developed by theorists such as John Dewey.

[15]The **Plowden Report** is the unofficial name for the 1967 **report** of the Central Advisory Council For Education (England) into Primary education in England. The **report**, entitled Children and their Primary Schools reviewed Primary education in a wholesale fashion.

Selection for secondary education (the 'eleven-plus') was being abolished, freeing primary schools from the constraints imposed by the need to 'get good results'. Streaming (sorting children into classes on the basis of ability or overall intelligence) was being abandoned. Marshall (1963) was writing about the creativity of primary pupils in 'An Experiment in Education'. Comprehensive schools and middle schools were being established. Teacher-led curriculum innovation was being actively encouraged. Plowden was very much a product of its time, full of enthusiasm and optimism.

(http://www.infed.org/schooling/plowden_report.htm, accessed 27th May 2016).

Here was a language and a framework of perception which represented the learner differently, indeed which brought learning to the fore, which raised questions about the curriculum as an experience, and encouraged the teacher to reflect on their purpose and practice in the classroom. Here the teacher was being formed in a relation to practice rather than simply within practice. Pedagogy became a matter of deliberation and judgement rather than a pre-given relation to the student. As Henriques et al. (2005, p. 164) put it, 'progressivism was at once made possible by specific sciences but was the result of a 'precarious congruence' (Donald 1979, p. 17) in which regulation, classification and liberation coexisted as simultaneous possibilities.

This simultaneity and what Gillard calls the liberal context, may be seen more generally as part of what Bernstein calls 'the social logic' of *competence* (Bernstein 1996, p. 55), which was, he suggests, evident in 'a remarkable convergence [that] took place in the field of the social and psychological sciences' (p. 54) in the 1960s. He sums this logic up as: 'An inbuilt procedural democracy, an in-built creativity, an in-built virtuous self-regulation' (p. 56). This was an intellectual field, he argues, 'whose authors had little or no initial connection with education, came to play such a central role in the theory and practice of education' (p. 57)[16]—Piaget is key to education here. This is where I suggest the expertise of the teacher was produced, within this intellectual field, however uncertainly, and as it turned out temporarily.[17] Bernstein asserts that 'competence modes became dominant positions in the PRF [pedagogical recontextualisation field—teacher education, educational research and educational media] in the late 1960s' (1996, p. 70), institutionalised in England by the publication of the Plowden report (1969) *Children: Their Primary Schools*. Perhaps in Foucault's terms, this is a new 'intellectual subconscious' for education, a shift in the possibilities of pedagogical knowledge, within which the relation of the teacher to student and what it means to teach and to learn are re-designated.

---

[16]To some extent Foucault was part of this new logic and his writing contributed to liberatory moves especially as it was taken up within the anti-psychiatry movement.

[17]Bernstein goes on to adumbrate a set of variations or modes within the general model (progressive, populist and radical)—I am interested in the model rather than the modes here. But he says all three share a preoccupation with the development, the recognition and change of consciousness (p. 68). He goes on in this chapter, again with resonances of Foucault to discuss the relationship of pedagogy, to *transitional capitalism* and the concomitant 'possibility of new identity constructions' (p. 76).

What was involved here was a shift from the student as producer and performer, to the 'whole child', a shift from measuring and representing the child, to knowing the child, from a form of pedagogy that is based on transmission to one that is focused on acquisition– tellingly in Bernstein's terms from *visible* to *invisible*, from surface to depth. And there is a concomitant shift away from biological to cultural explanations of failure or difference, from fixity—based 'upon the realization of competences that acquirers already possess or are thought to possess' (1996, p. 58) —to possibility, articulated in part through psychological accounts of development and different stages and rates of development. That is, a shift to attuning pedagogy to the child (invisible) rather than the child to pedagogy (visible).

The constitution of the child as a developmental (developing) subject, positions the teacher in relation to the child as judge (what stage are they at?) and nurturer/pedagogue (how can I move them on?). At the same time this detaches classroom practice from its direct and subordinate relation to the selection and sequencing and assessment of knowledge. The examination is rendered redundant, assessment becomes a formative tool rather than a summative classification. At the same time this detachment opened up possibilities for new kinds of power relations and political practices. In real terms these latter possibilities were taken up, if at all, in very few schools and classrooms (RisingHill,[18] William Tyndale,[19] Holland Park[20]) and the precarious concatenation of this social logic and new liberalism and liberation was to be swiftly and brutally disassembled.

To some extent at least, invisible pedagogy dissolves the formal division of space and time, and the authority of the teacher, that are fundamental to the disciplinary school, and thus 'a pedagogic practice of this type is (at least initially) invisible to the acquirer, essentially because the acquirer appears to fill the pedagogic space rather than the transmitter' (Bernstein 1990, p. 71). And crucially the celebration and ordering of organisational differences (age, ability, category) is replaced by a celebration of individual differences and *uniqueness* rather than comparison; 'Invisible pedagogies are less concerned to produce explicit stratifying differences between acquirers because they are apparently less interested in matching the acquirer's text against an external common standard' (p. 71). In Foucault's words 'life has left the tabulated space of order and become wild once more' (1970, p. 277). The norm recedes from view—acquisition rather than performance is emphasised and *sequencing rules* of acquisition are displaced. What Bernstein suggests is that what he calls the *grammar* or *ordering principles* of pedagogic practice are different in each case—that is 'general principles underlying

---

[18]See http://www.libed.org.uk/index.php/articles/348-risinghill-revisited.

[19]'This book chronicles the teachers' (of WT) attempt to make their school a more open and humane institution, a place where the children could learn to take an active and responsible role in their own education, and where the teachers could decide in democratic ways on their methods of work' (Back cover *William Tyndale The teachers' story* (1976) Readers and writers Publishing Cooperative.

[20]See https://www.theguardian.com/news/2007/aug/25/guardianobituaries.obituaries, on Holland Park's first Headteacher Allen Clarke.

the transformation of knowledge into pedagogic communication '(Bernstein 1996, p. 39), where such communication is a 'carrier, a relay for ... external power relations' (p. 39).

Nonetheless, there are two stings in the Bernsteinian tail, which bring us back to Foucault, or a slightly different, later Foucault.[21] First, Bernstein suggests the assumptions and competencies 'available in the family and the child' (1996, p. 84), required by invisible pedagogies 'are less likely to be met in class or ethnically disadvantaged groups, and as a consequence ... the teacher is likely to misread the cultural and cognitive significance of the child' (p. 84). A new form of differentiation and categorisation is evoked. Secondly, in the 'multi-layering of communication' required by invisible pedagogies there is a weakening of the division 'between the inside of the child and the outside ... More of the child's feelings, fantasies, fears and aspirations are expected to be made public. The surveillance of the child is total' (p. 83). This is the 'pathology' of the invisible pedagogy. An intensification of power if you like, as the whole child is opened up to the *expert* pedagogic gaze of the teacher, a teacher who now does not differentiate the child on the basis of outward indicators of performance but understands the child in terms of their interior differences. It is within the subtle and conditional temporalities of development that childhood and the pupil are 'made up', and normalized, by what MacNaughton (2005, p. 30) calls 'officially sanctioned developmental truths of the child'. Henriques et al. (2005, p. 195) make a similar argument about progressive pedagogy; 'such a model' they say 'assumes a psychological subject laid bare to be re-formed in the new order' (and) 'such psychology and such practices are normalising in that they constitute a mode of observation and surveillance of production of children. Given this, it is difficult to conceive of these practices as being the basis of any kind of pedagogy which could potentially "liberate" children' (p. 195). Allen also makes this point:

> The history of the monitorial school must be placed alongside its rival, the moral training school, which inaugurated an educational tradition in which 'free play' and 'democratic accountability' entered the educational landscape. This tradition makes a virtue of pedagogies that pay attention to the natural environment and dispositions of the child. The child is located, very explicitly, at the centre of a moral scheme that is just as pernicious, if not more so, due to the skill by which it conceals its activities. To prioritize and listen to the child, to respond to the child, in the child's own terms, embeds the child more firmly in a framework of power that has become so widespread that it is barely perceived.

> (see   http://socialtheoryapplied.com/2013/04/17/foucault-disciplinary-power-and-the-dangerous-remainder/, accessed 7.3.16).

Foucault also identifies an earlier iteration of progressivism and developmentalism.

> We find the mould, the first model of the pedagogical colonisation of youth, in this practice of the individual's exercise on himself, this attempt to transform the individual, this search

---

[21]Bernstein acknowledges the possibility of a relation of his analysis to Foucault in Chap. 3 (1996, p. 54) of PSCI.

for a progressive development of the individual up to the point of salvation, in this ascetic
work of the individual on himself for his own salvation. On the basis of this, and in the
collective form of this asceticism in the Brothers of the Common Life, we see the great
schemas of pedagogy taking shape, that is to say, the idea that one can learn things only by
passing through a number of obligatory and necessary stages, that these stages follow each
other in time, and that in this ordered movement through time, each stage represents a
degree of progress. The twinning of time and progress is typical of ascetic practice, and it
will be equally typical of pedagogical practice. (Foucault 2006b, p. 67)

It is possible to see here then an intensification of power, embedded in the
paradox discussed by Bernstein. While the modern school, as a form of panopticon,
is premised upon and enacts a vertical and oppressive model of power, very evident
in *Discipline and Punish*. The progressive school is premised on the sort of
transversal (Foucault 2001, p. 239) and relational version of power outlined in
History of Sexuality Volume 1 (1981), which is more labile and mobile but no less
effective in the constitution of subjectivity.[22] As Lazaroiu (2013, p. 822) puts it:
'Modern pedagogies are secular technologies of the self in which self-regulation
and self-examination occupy centre ground'.

Embedded in the power/knowledge couplet, in education and elsewhere, is a
paradox—a contradiction between knowing and being 'known', between competence and domination. Deacon notes that 'What particularly intrigued Foucault,
even though he did not develop this insight, was the problem of knowing how, in
the typical pedagogical relationship, to avoid the effects of domination' (2006,
p. 184). In the enactment of judgement and the practices of evaluation and comparison, particular kinds of truth[23]—the truths told about us—articulate our 'discursive currency' (Prado 2006, p. 80). That is, ways of thinking and talking about
ourselves, to ourselves and to others—'a regime of truth offers the terms that make
self-recognition possible' (Butler 2005, p. 22). This as Foucault puts it, is the face
of truth which has been 'turned away from us for so long and which is that of its
violence' (2013, p. 4).

Crucially, for my argument, within all of this 'the teacher operates with a theory
of reading' (Bernstein 1996, p. 61) within which 'the meaning of an acquirer's
signs is not available to the acquirer, only to the teacher' (p. 61) and 'this marks the
professionalism of the teacher' (p. 61). Here at last is recourse to esoteric knowledge. 'Meaning is no longer read in an immediate perception, the figure no longer
speaks for itself' (Foucault 2001, p. 16). But contra Foucault it is not testing and
'the examination [that] enabled the teacher, while transmitting his knowledge, to
transform his pupils into a whole field of knowledge' (Foucault 1979, p. 186) but
rather the absence of the examination and indeed the test and the 'freedom' of the
learner, which produces a space of observation, interpretation and perception for the
teacher as pedagogue. It is within progressive pedagogies that the body of the

---

[22]I will come back to this shift in Foucault's conceptualization of power in Chap. 3.

[23]Foucault does not offer a definition of truth; rather he provides a multi-faceted characterization
(Prado 2006, p. 81).

learner is now 'offered up to new forms of knowledge' (1979, p. 155) within the classroom and 'a whole analytical pedagogy was being formed' (1979, p. 159).

Neoliberal Pedagogy

Paradoxically, the subsequent suppression or subjugation of progressive pedagogies, without any other claims to esoteric knowledge, leave the teacher exposed to and susceptible to a new and different kind of fabrication. What had vaguely and fragilely emerged in the period of the welfare state after the WW2 as the professional teacher, a teacher with an independent and scientific claim to judgement, is in the post-welfare period, a new historical conjuncture, a problem rather than a resource. The emphasis on care, on individuality, on 'knowing' the learner in their individuality, over and against taxonomy and typology, on understanding rather than managing behaviour, and the relation of that to the differentiation of learning experiences over and against the differentiation of students, and the avoidance of measurement—examinations or tests—is not well aligned to the needs of the neoliberal competition state and the evolving neoliberal economy. The classroom has been brought back into a direct and very visible relation to docility and productivity and security. The classroom door has been forced open once more to enable the tying of the school every more directly to the accumulation of capital (see Foucault 1979, p. 221). However, in this case it is a marketised, entrepreneurial school, formed in relation to the logic of competition, between students, teachers, schools and writ large between nations, through the techniques of international testing, and in relation to that, in the global economy.

So here there is a reversal or return of a kind, a re-emergence of a liberal politics, in neoliberal form, and in the classroom a renewed emphasis on managing behaviour and the fostering and celebrating performance over competence—but in relation to different labour market relations and economic and security relations. There is a return to enumeration and examination—via league tables, benchmarks, and targets. The development of new forms of measurement, articulated in relation to new ways of governing. This is what we might call *neoliberal pedagogy*, the 'technocratic embedding of routines of neoliberal governance' (Peck and Tickell 2002) in the everyday life of the school and the classroom.

This entails the dissolution of an esoteric basis for pedagogical knowledge, for teaching, and opens the classroom up to another transition, another kind of fracturing. A rupture in which the school is no longer set alongside and in resemblance to other institutions of the welfare state and the needs of the management of the population at least in the form that Foucault (1979) suggests—'Is it surprising that prisons resemble factories, schools, barracks, hospitals, which all resemble prisons?' (1979, p. 228)—but rather is reconstituted in resemblance to 'the firm' and the needs of the economy and efficiency and cost and the management of the workforce,[24] productivity rather than docility.[25]

> * "Everything gets measured and what gets measured gets managed" McKinsey in-house motto.

That is, 'the extension of the economic form of the market 'to the entire social body and to generalize it inside the whole social system that, normally, does not pass through or is not authorized by the market' (Foucault 2010, p. 248). Here the separation of learning from adult life, and its simulation in schools, what Foucault somewhat confusingly calls the 'pedagogization of learning' becomes much less clear-cut.

> When, with Rousseau and Pestalozzi, the eighteenth century concerned itself with constituting for the child, with educational rules that followed his development, a world that would be adapted to him, it made it possible to form around children an unreal, abstract, archaic environment that had no relation to the adult world. The whole development of contemporary education, with its irreproachable aim of preserving the child from adult conflicts, accentuates the distance that separates, for a man, his life as a child and his life as an adult. That is to say, by sparing the child conflicts, it exposes him to a major conflict, to the contradiction between his childhood and his real life. If one adds that, in its educational institutions, a culture does not project its reality directly, with all its conflicts and contradictions, but that it reflects it indirectly through the myths that excuse it, justify it, and idealize it in a chimerical coherence; if one adds that in its education a society dreams of its golden age [...] one understands that fixations and pathological regressions are possible only in a given culture, that they multiply to the extent that social forms do not permit the assimilation of the past into the present content of experience. (Foucault 1987, p. 81)

The 'deeper' esoteric knowledges of the child have been once again re-located from the classroom into the specialized functions of educational psychology, with its new forms of testing and new *taxinomia*—dyslexia, ADHD etc.—and neuroscience (Gillborn 2016) (see below).

As far as the teacher and the classroom is concerned the disciplines and discipline have become detached. The disciplines have their most direct relation to policy, and thence and indirect relation to practice.[26] At the same time, developmentalism has become re-embedded in the logic of neoliberalism, led by supranational and international organisations emphasising the role of early childhood

---

[24]Although it is exactly in these terms, at a pervious historical conjuncture, that Foucault outlines the methods of *discipline* (1979, pp. 220–223).

[25]Nonetheless, of course, what is happening is that prisons and hospitals are also made subject to these reforms, which re-establishes a new resemblance between them, and between them and school.

[26]In October 2014, the Welcome Trust and Education Endowment Foundation (EEF) announced the launch of six projects to investigate a variety of ways in which neuroscience might improve teaching and learning in the UK. Thousands of pupils across England will take part in a series of randomised controlled trials after the funding bodies identified a need for more robust evidence about how neuroscience relates to learning in order to support teachers and schools keen to use the science. The six projects have been awarded grants totalling almost £4 million. http://www.cne.psychol.cam.ac.uk/news/educationneuroscience.

development and education in securing economic growth, which in turn, has begun to influence the ways in which national governments engage with early childhood through education and social policy. Children are constructed as resources, valuable to the extent that they become productive citizens in the future as human capital.

> The emphasis on human capital at an international level can be seen as evidence of hegemonic globalisation, whereby a series of universal truths have been created as to the benefits of early childhood education and care (ECEC). Human capital offers a powerful global rational for national governments to invest in ECEC provision and offers evidence of where localism was once valued in caring for young children, now global economics plays a part. (Campbell-Barr and Nygard 2014, p. 348).

There are other traces of reversal and return in relation to contemporary pedagogy. First, we might note the reassertion of the early modern teacher as a moral subject, a child saving subject—which is most evident in those programmes like Teach First (Bailey 2015) and Teaching Leaders, which significantly also are organised on the basis of a return to pre-state forms of philanthropic education, a return to a rhetoric of meritocracy, and to forms of training that emphasise the character of the teacher and their practical classroom management skills.

Mission

To address educational disadvantage by growing a movement of outstanding middle leaders in schools in challenging contexts.

Vision

Teaching Leaders' vision is of a better society: one where life chances are not predetermined by social class, nor shackled by educational disadvantage. In the belief that children's success at school can be driven not by social background but by the quality and kind of education they receive, we want to strengthen the capacity of those who lead teaching and learning closest to the action on the front-line of schools in challenging contexts: middle leaders.

Values

The work of Teaching Leaders is focused around achieving our mission and driven by our core values:

- **Uncompromising.** We believe that in order to achieve our mission, we have to do whatever it takes; maintain the highest expectations and standards, retain a culture of no excuses, and believe in a growth mind-set through which every middle leader and child can achieve their potential

- **Personal.** We know that development and learning is different for every individual, so we listen to their needs, respond to feedback and adapt the way we deliver to provide personalised support to allow everyone to succeed

- **Collaborative.** We have a shared moral purpose and our movement works best when it works together, sharing content and ideas, jointly developing practice and collaborating to collectively achieve our mission

- **Innovative.** We know the challenges we face often require new approaches and creative solutions but we believe in innovating in a disciplined way, basing interventions and approaches on evidence

- **Optimistic.** We remain relentlessly optimistic that we can improve the life outcomes of every child, which will in turn motivate others and create an unstoppable movement for change.

This return to a *pedagogy of morality* and its clear undertones of pastoralism is mirrored in a renewed emphasis on the character and resilience of the student.

> The definition of character in major research reports and Department for Education statements and support materials is broad. It includes 'therapeutic' approaches that are associated with the policy emphasis on well being as well as more 'traditional' approaches to character that specify virtues and character traits. It is a blended and **flexible** approach … It is also interesting to note that in allowing this flexibility, there has been an increasing emphasis on 'performance virtues' such as grit and resilience.

This has not gone unnoticed by the Jubilee Centre- a major research Centre and provider of materials and receiver of funding- who express concern about an undue emphasis on 'Performance Virtues' rather than 'Moral Virtues' such as courage and honesty. (Jones 2016)

Furthermore, as noted above, in an odd relation to morality, there is also a return to the late modern preoccupation with biological explanations of differences in performance but in this case neuroscience and epigenetics.

The Department of Educational Neuroscience, Faculty of Psychology and Education of the Vrije University of Amsterdam will be hosting the 4th biennial meeting of the Special Interest Group (SIG) 22 "Neuroscience and Education" of the European Association for Research on Learning and Instruction (EARLY) (http://www.sig22neuroeducation.com)/2016-conference.html)

Biosocial explanations of phenomenon are becoming prevalent in the public policy arena, specifically as 'biosocial justifications for governmental intervention' (Pykett and Disney 2015). This combination of academic study and policy-use produce an emerging set of implications relating to new developments in life sciences and raise questions concerning, for example, citizenship, subjectivity and policy-making and the desired introjections or 'implementations' of biosocial solutions to problems previously considered to be entirely social in nature … (Gulson and Webb 2016).

Alongside testing and the examination, the possibilities of categorisation and the scourge of the norm, Allen (2014) illustrates the continuing role of eugenic rationality within contemporary education. He reminds us of the tortuous but fundamental intertwining of eugenics, testing and the *Origin of the Species*—the survival of the fittest, the need to adapt to changing environmental conditions—meritocracy in other words. Meritocracy, a term rediscovered and laughably misunderstood by Tony Blair, is now to the forefront of many of the third sector programmes that are embedded in English education policy—like Teach First, the Sutton Trust and ARK, whose *raison d'etre* is to identify and sponsor the aspiring, able and deserving children of the working class. This works through what Allen (2014, p. 189) calls systems of *extraction*. This is a 'charitable' focus that Francis Galton, founder of intelligence testing, argued for in the 19th century (p. 99) based on a division between what he termed 'desirables', 'passables', and 'undesirables'.

Eugenics works by combining 'scientific testing' with systems of categories which then also define the limits of normality. There are now developments underway to extend the remit of testing from intelligence to character, DEMOS, the Blairian think tank, is one of several organisations jostling for the money attached to the current focus on character education championed by Nicky Morgan (England's Secretary of State for Education July 2014-July 2016) and others (http://www.demos.co.uk/projects/the-character-inquiry). Character is was already firmly embedded in UK Conservative Party welfare policy, with its fundamental division between strivers and skivers[27]—the latter who threaten a 'deterioration in the noblest part of our nature' (Darwin's *The Descent of Man 1871*, p. 90). As Allen says 'The success of eugenics would rely heavily on its popular appeal' (2014, p. 107) and that continues to be the case as eugenic claims appear regularly in ministerial statements and tabloid headlines.

Within all of this there is a re-fabrication of the teacher as technician rather than as professional, through a proliferation of schemes, programmes and methods, which the teacher is expected to 'follow' and use (and 'make their own')—like, for example, Maths Mastery.

> We have created an integrated professional development structure that flows seamlessly into every aspect of delivering outstanding mathematics teaching.
>
> One-off training days rarely make a long-term difference. When you return to the classroom, the pressures of preparing lessons and delivering classes can mean the ideas from training can go out the window. That's why we provide continued support, to ensure teachers have all of the training and resources required to teach every lesson over the course of the year.
>
> This process begins with face-to-face workshops, where we impart the principles of Mathematics Mastery to partner teachers. This gives teachers the understanding, skills and frameworks to begin applying Mathematics Mastery in their classrooms. We then provide ongoing coaching and mentoring, as well as school visits, from experienced trainers to support teachers in their development. This is reinforced with access to exclusive online teaching and learning materials, including lesson guides for each week.
>
> These guides give ideas and techniques for teachers to use in their lessons, integrating formal training with daily practice. They are not made to save time, but to allow teachers to spend more time creating and adapting lessons and using professional development training modules.
>
> Mathematics Mastery also encourages teachers to use this framework to develop their own lessons and teaching techniques. Nothing delights us more than teachers absorbing the support and resources we provide and making them their own. (http://mathematicsmastery. cheeselab.co.uk/our-vision/integrated-professional-development/).

There is here also a new response to the current political and economic conjuncture, in relation to the changing form and modalities of the state, and changing boundaries between the economy and the state. That is, the re-positioning of education in many different respects as an opportunity for profit or social enterprise. The thorough re-working of the school as an enterprising institution, within which the 'cost' of the teacher is a problem to be solved, and the professionalism of the teacher, is a problem to be overcome.

A business model of schooling and its sensibilities and concomitant budgetary concerns lead to a focus on issues of cost, and foremost among school costs are teacher salaries; driving down wage costs can take the form of reducing the number of teachers, by introducing Edtech pedagogies, like *blended learning*; and/or deregulating teacher certification and employment, or by employing non-qualified

---

[27]See   https://www.theguardian.com/commentisfree/2015/jun/23/skivers-strivers-200-year-old-myth-wont-die.

teachers and/or training 'in house' and a reliance on 'what works'. These new forms of teacher employment often involve a shift to non-union labour and a preference for enterprising/innovative teacher subjects, untrammelled by welfare sensibilities; concomitantly systems and practices are introduced that ensure teacher labour and organizational decision-making are closely related to student performance indicators, which bring into play various forms of performance management, like, as mentioned previously, performance-related pay (and the dismissal of poorly performing teachers). This outcome data, usually generated and managed using measurement software systems, is used also as a form of self-promotion both in relation to student recruitment and institutional competition.

Clearly, again the move from progressive to neoliberal pedagogy is not a clean break; there is an overlaying of new upon old forms of power, a re-working of knowledges, practices and techniques within different conditions of possibility. The point of application of these techniques is, as Allen (2014, p. 224) carefully points out, now different, rather than the 19th century concern with altering the normal distribution of outcomes, 'the rate of individual progression … is the focus of improvement', articulated through 'value-added' measurements. As he goes on to say the proliferation of base-line testing and student performance monitoring systems has also generated new business opportunities for universities and businesses eager to sell their systems to institutions insatiable for 'process-based technologies' (p. 231)—here neoliberal academia can seek both impact and profit. Testing and monitoring work at the nexus between aspiration, hope and failure—schools now predict futures, manipulate hope, and produce 'likely futures' (p. 233).

The intertwining of discipline with governmentality, a shift from docility to productivity, from discipline to enterprise, is not then an absolute shift but one of emphasis. A shift which reflects and responds to Foucault's adumbration of another phase in the genealogy of the state—the emergence of the neoliberal state, and the concomitant rearticulation of the school as a site for the construction of neoliberal subjectivities—no longer is there a break between the world of education and the real world, rather the school, and education more generally are made subject to the extension of the economic form of the market. We can think of this in relation to the change of emphasis in Foucault's concerns with truth, power and subjectivity, from the foregrounding of power in *Discipline and Punish* to the foregrounding of subjectivity in *The Birth of Biopolitics*. Perhaps also this is a shift from the first part to the second part of his oft quoted formulation of the subject 'subject to someone else by control and dependence, and tied to his own identity by a conscience or self-knowledge. Both meanings suggest a form of power which subjugates and makes subject to' (Foucault 1982, p. 212).

Neoliberalism is a rationality of government that relies in very particular ways on a 'political anatomy of the body'. This is a new iteration of the population as a resource within which individuals, institutions and states must be 'lean', 'fit' and flexible, and indeed agile—active citizens in an active society. Here bodies are not 'docile' rather they are engaged in a form of insidious 'disciplined self-management' (Ozga 2009, p. 152) which involves making themselves healthy, 'ready', adaptable and agentic, in relation to the needs of fast capitalism, while at the same time, as 'biological citizens', taking responsibility for the damage that capital does. This is a 'remoralisation' of our relation to the state and to ourselves (Peters 2001, pp. 59–60). 'It aspires to construct a responsible and moral individual … whose moral quality is based on the fact that they rationally assess the costs and benefits of a certain act…' (Lemke 2000, p. 12). The research on parental choice, for example, exemplifies this kind of responsible and assiduous individualism in contemporary education. This is the ontology of neo-liberalism: '… The only real agents, must be individuals, or let's say, if you like enterprises' (Foucault 2010 p. 173).

Having said that, education policy and practice, certainly in the contemporary period, are hybridized and incoherent. We systematic write the school as a one-dimensional site of power, as too modern, too neoliberal and neglect the intersection of forms of power. Nonetheless, we might seriously consider whether contemporary pedagogies, at least in part, are a form of neoliberal education, are part of a neoliberal *dispositif*, in which is constituted specific kinds of learner subjects who are adapted to risk, economic uncertainty and austerity.

Foucault as Anti-educator: Humanism and Education: Is Education Possible in Foucault?

I have sought to deconstruct the teacher, using Foucault to demonstrate the absence of a science of pedagogy in education or at least in the classroom. In relation to the constitution of the school as a site of power, of management and of economic efficiency, teachers are, essentially, 'technicians of behaviour', or 'engineers of conduct' (Foucault 1979 p. 294). Man—in this case as teacher and learner, says Foucault, in an aside which links together his archeological and genealogical analyses and their periodisations; 'is, after all … as he was thought and [and] defined by the nineteenth century's so-called human sciences and as he was reflected in nineteenth-century humanism nothing more, ultimately, than a figure of population' (Foucault 2009, p. 81). There is nothing very original in all of that. In chapter three I will explore the possibility of reconstructing the teacher as a very different kind of ethical subject.

So what does this tell us about Foucault and education or Foucault as educator. In the most obvious sense the recurring issue for Foucault is 'whether an increase in our capabilities must necessarily be purchased at the price of our intensified subjection' (Burchell 1996, p. 34) and thus the impossibility (and necessity) of education. The more we learn, the more we are made subject. Here education is straightforwardly a grid of power. As Green (1998, pp. 197–198) puts it, viewed from Foucault's perspective education is nothing more than: 'An imaginary field linking nostalgia and desire, including social anxieties around questions of change and generation, language and authority, structure and freedom, discipline and order'.

Here is one version of Foucault's anti-humanism, a denunciation both of foun-
dationalism and of an Enlightenment-inspired, progressivist view of history, as the
result of the actions of autonomous agents. One of the persistent and fundamental
themes of his thought is his critique of the 'anthropologism' of modern thought, the
tendency that is to equate knowledge as such with human knowledge, truth with
human truth—the extraction of transcendental truth from an empirical being—in
The Archaeology of Knowledge he described his project as one in which history
would be 'untied from all anthropological constraints … purified of any anthropologism' (1974, p. 25) and anthropocentric notions such as an essential subject. As
Leask (2011, p. 58) puts it 'for Foucault, the post-Enlightenment world is char-
acterized, not so much by the increased civilization and progress of its self-image
but by an ever-widening (yet always anonymous) range of processes, techniques
and technologies designed to ensure a regularized, efficient and docile social
whole'—or as argued above active social whole. The school is one of many sites at
which 'the doctrine of ontological individualism' (Olssen 2006, p. 177) is played
out. Foucault rails against 'medical humanism' in *The Birth of the Clinic*, and we
can perhaps imagine him, pouring derision, sarcasm and moral indignation in a
similar way on both progressive educators and those bourgeois moralists who seek
through education to make the working classes 'responsible'.

Leask (2011, p. 59) goes on to say 'Overall, Foucauldian analysis can now strip
away the myths and self-deceit of educators, and expose the grim truth of the
education process—namely, that it is a core element in the mechanics of modern
disciplinarity' (p. 59). Foucault seeks to dispense with the Enlightenment faith in
subject-centred reason. Education is not a site of reason but rather a site of discipline and discourse and differentiation, not simply reproduction, and certainly not
liberation or discovery. Rather than seeing education and schooling (although we
may want to separate these out) as means by which the individual is enabled to
develop or unfold toward some absolute form of rational being, it is the conditions
and contexts within which individuals are produced and made up that is important.
'The individual subject is a reality fabricated by … discipline (Foucault 1979,
p. 194). Therefore, 'it is not so much that "we go to school"; it is more that we only
emerge from school' (Leask 2011 p. 60).[28] Man is 'already in himself the effect of a
subjection' (Foucault 1979, p. 30). Surely there are enough asides in *Discipline and
Punish* to indicate that education is one of those 'monsters' that Foucault's work
addresses and condemns (or would have), this may seem 'over the top', extreme,
but that is part of his style and method of working, part of his *limit attitude* and his
irony toward the present. This is the kind of analysis that underlies Illich's (1976)
argument for the need to 'de-school society'.[29]

---

[28]See Grant (1997).

[29]Interestingly, in relation to pastoral power, Illich draws a parallel between the medieval priest
and the promise of life after death and the modern teacher promising life after school.

References

Allen, A. (2014). *Benign violence: Education in and beyond the age of reason.* Basingstoke: Palgrave Macmillan.

Bailey, P. L. J. (2015). *"Teach First" as a dispositif: Towards a critical ontology of policy and power.* London: Institute of Education, University of London.

Ball, S. J. (2001). Performativities and fabrications in the education economy: Towards the performative society. In D. Gleeson & C. Husbands (Eds.), *The performing school: Managing teaching and learning in a performance culture.* London: RoutledgeFalmer.

Ball, S. J. (2013). *Foucault, power and education.* London and New York: Routledge.

Barr, R. B., & Tagg, J. (1995). From teaching to learning—A new paradigm for undergraduate education. *Change: The Magazine Of Higher Learning, 27*(6), 12–26.

Bernstein, B. (1990). *The structuring of pedagogic discourse.* London: Routledge.

Bernstein, B. (1996). *Pedagogy symbolic control and identity.* London: Taylor and Francis.

Besley, T. (2005). Foucault, truth telling and technologies of the self in schools. *Journal of Educational Enquiry, 6*(1), 76–89.

Burchell, G. (1996). Liberal government and techniques of the self. In A. Barry, T. Osborne, & N. Rose (Eds.), *Foucault and political reason.* London: UCL Press.

Butler, J. (2005). *Giving an account of oneself.* New York: Fordham University Press.

Campbell-Barr, V., & Nygard, M. (2014). Losing sight of the child? Human capital theory and its role for early childhood education and care policies in Finland and England since the mid-1990s. *Contemporary Issues in Early Childhood, 15*(4), 346–359.

Deacon, R. (2006). From confinement to attachment: Michel foucault on the rise of the school. *The European Legacy, 11*(2), 121–138.

Dean, M. (2007). *Governing societies: Political perspectives on domestic and international rule.* Maidenhead: Open University Press.

Dean, M. (2010). *Governmentality: Power and rule in modern society.* London: Sage.

Deleuze, G. (1995). Gilles Deleuze's interview on Foucault, 'life as a work of art'. In *Negotiations: 1972–1990* (pp. 94–101) (Martin Joughin, trans.). New York: Columbia University Press

Devine-Eller, A. (2004). *Applying foucault to education.* http://issuu.com/gfbertini/docs/applying_foucault_to_education

Donald, J. (1992). *Sentimental education: Schooling, popular culture and the regulation of liberty.* New York: Verso.

Dreyfus, H. L., & Rabinow, P. (1983). *Michel Foucault: Beyond structuralism and hermeneutics* (2nd ed.). Chicago: University of Chicago Press.

Edwards, R. (2002). Mobilizing lifelong learning: Governmentality in educational practices. *Journal of Education Policy, 17*(3), 353–365.

Evans, J. E. R., & Holroyd, R. (2004). Disordered eating and disordered schooling: what schools to do middle class girls. *British Journal of Sociology of Education, 25*(2), 123–142.

Floud, J., & Halsey, A. H. (1961). Social class, intelligence tests and selection for secondary schools. In: A. H. Halsey, J. Floud, & C. A. Anderson (Eds.), *Education, economy and society.* New York: Free Press.

Flynn, T. R. (2005). *Satre, Foucault and Historical Reason Vol 2: A poststructuralist mapping of history.* Chicago: University of Chicago Press.

Foucault, M. (1970). *The order of things.* New York: Pantheon.

Foucault, M. (1972). *The archeology of knowledge.* New York: Vintage.

Foucault, M. (1974). *The archaeology of knowledge.* London: Tavistock.

Foucault, M. (1979). *Discipline and punish.* Harmondsworth: Peregrine.

Foucault, M. (1980). *Power/knowledge: Selected interviews and other writings.* New York: Pantheon.

Foucault, M. (1981). *The history of sexuality: An introduction.* Harmondsworth: Penguin.

Foucault, M. (1982). The subject and power: Afterword to. In H. Dreyfus & P. Rabinow (Eds.), *Michel Foucault: Beyond structuralism and hermeneutics*. Chicago: University of Chicago Press.

Foucault, M. (1984). Neitzsche, genealogy, history. In P. Rabinow (Ed.), *The Foucault reader*. London: Peregrine.

Foucault, M. (1987). *Mental illness and psychology*. Berkeley: University of California Press.

Foucault, M. (2001). *Madness and civilization*. London: Routledge.

Foucault, M. (2004). *Society must be defended*. London: Penguin Books.

Foucault, M. (2006a). *History of madness*. London: Routledge.

Foucault, M. (2006b). *Psychiatric power: Lectures at the Collège de France, 1973–1974*. Basingstoke: Palgrave Macmillan.

Foucault, M. (2009). *Security, territory, population: Lectures at the College de France 1977–78*. New York: Palgrave Macmillan.

Foucault, M. (2010). *The Birth of Biopolitics: Lectures at the College de France 1978–1979*. Basingstoke: Palgrave Macmillan.

Gallagher, M. (2010). Are schools panoptic? *Surveillance and Society, 7*(3–4), 262–272.

Gillborn, D. (2016). Softly, softly: Genetics, intelligence and the hidden racism of the new geneism. *Journal of Education Policy*, http://dx.doi.org/10.1080/02680939.2016.1139189

Golder, B. (2009). Foucault and the genealogy of pastoral power. *Radical Philosophy Review, 10*(2), 157–176.

Gordon, C. (1991). Governmental rationality: An introduction. In G. Burchell, C. Gordon, & P. Miller (Eds.), *The Foucault effect: Studies in governmentality*. Harvester/Wheatsheaf: Brighton.

Gore, J. (1997). Power relations in pedagogy: Am empirical study based on Foucauldian thought. In C. O'Farrell (Ed.), *Foucault: The legacy*. Bisbane: Queensland University of Technology.

Grant, B. (1997). Disciplining students: The construction of student subjectivities. *British Journal of Sociology of Education, 18*, 101–114.

Green, B. (1998). Born-again teaching? governmentality, "grammar" and public schooling. In T. S. Popkewitz & M. Brennan (Eds.), *Foucault's challenge: Discourse, knowledge and power in education*. New York: Teachers College Press.

Gulson, K. N., & Webb, P. T. (2016). The new biological rationalities for education policy: (Molecular) biopolitics and governing the future. In S. Parker, K. N. Gulson, & T. Gale (Eds.), *Education policy and social inequality*. Dordrecht: Springer.

Henriques, J., Hollway, W., Urwin, C., Venn, C., & Walkerdine, V. (2005). *Changing the subject: Psychology, social regulation and subjectivity*. London and New York: Routledge.

Hook, D. (2007). *Foucault, psychology and the analytics of power*. Basingstoke: Palgrave MacMillan.

Hope, A. (2015). Biopower and school surveillance technologies 2.0. *British Journal of Sociology of Education*.

Hoskin, K. (1990). Foucault under examination: The crypto-educationalist unmasked. In S. J. Ball (Ed.), *Foucault and education: Disciplines and knowledge*. London: Routledge.

Hunter, I. (1996). Assembling the school. In A. Barry, T. Osborne, & N. Rose (Eds.), *Foucault and political reason: Liberalism, neo-liberalism and rationalities of government*. London: UCL Press.

Jones, B. (2016). *Thesis is progress: A genealogy of the whole child*. London: University College London.

Jones, D. (1990). The genealogy of the urban schoolteacher. In S. J. Ball (Ed.), *Foucault and education: Disciplines and knowledge*. London: Routledge.

Larsen, M. A. (2011). *The making and shaping of the Victorian Teacher: A comparative new cultural history*. Basingstoke: Palgrave Macmillan.

Lazaroiu, G. (2013). Besley on Foucault's discourse of education. *Educational Philosophy and Theory, 45*(8), 821–832.

Leask, I. (2011). Beyond subjection: Notes on the later Foucault and education. *Educational Philosophy and Theory, 44*(1), 57–73.

Lemke, T. (2000). Foucault, governmentality, and critique. Paper Presented at the Rethinking Marxism Conference, University of Amherst (MA). http://www.andosciasociology.net/resources/Foucault$2C+Governmentality$2C+and+Critique+IV-2.pdf

MacNaughton, G. (2005). *Doing Foucault in early childhood studies: Applying poststructural ideas*. London: Routledge.

Martin, L. H., Gutman, H., & Hutton, P. H. (Eds.). (1988). *Technologies of the self: A seminar with Michel Foucault*. London: Tavistock.

Nealon, J. T. (2008). *Foucault Beyond Foucault*. Stanford: Stanford University Press.

Olssen, M. (1993). Science and Individualism in educational psychology: Problems for practice and points of departure. *Educational Psychology, 13*(2), 155–172.

Olssen, M. (2006). Michel Foucault: *Materialism and education*, Boulder and London: Paradigm Press.

Ozga, J. (2009). Governing education through data in England: From regulation to self evaluation. *Journal of Education Policy, 24*(2), 149–162.

Peck, J., & Tickell, A. (2002). Neoliberalizing space. *Antipode, 34*(3), 380–404.

Perryman, J. (2006). Panoptic performativity and school inspection regimes: Disciplinary mechanisms and life under special measures. *Journal of Education Policy, 21*(2), 147–161.

Peters, M. (2001). Education, enterprise culture and the entrepreneurial self: A Foucualdian perspective. *Journal of Educational Enquiry, 2*(2), 58–71.

Popkewitz, T. (1998). *Struggling for the soul: The politics of schooling and the construction of the teacher*. New York: Teachers College Press.

Prado, C. G. (2006). *Searle and foucault on truth*. Cambridge: Cambridge University Press.

Pykett, J., & Disney, T. (2015). Brain-Targeted Teaching and the Biopolitical Child. In K. P. Kallio, & S. Mills (Eds.), *Politics, citizenship and rights*, Vol. 7 of Skelton, T. (ed.) Geographies of Children and Young People. Springer: Berlin.

Rose, N. (1999). *Powers of freedom: Reframing political thought*. Cambridge: Cambridge University Press.

Rose, N., & Miller, P. (1992). Political power beyond the state: Problematics of Government. *British Journal of Sociology, 43*(2), 173–205.

Scheer, A. (2011). Designed to control, destined to fail? Disciplinary practices at an inner-city elementary school in the United States. *Childhoods Today, 5*(2)

Sharp, R., & Green, T. (1975). *Education and social control*. London: Routledge and Kegan Paul.

Stoler, A. L. (1995). *Race and the education of desire: Foucault's history of sexuality and the colonial order of things*. Durham: Duke University Press.

Tate, T. (1857). The philosophy of education, Boston: Hickling, Swan and Brewer.

Chapter 2
Education as Critique—'Un-thinking' Education

Abstract This chapter asks—what can we learn from Foucault the teacher, the intellectual? How can we use Foucault to uneducate ourselves? It answers that we are invited to learn an attitude, a method, a relation to our own historicity, and our existence within and in relation to power. We are invited to learn the possibility of modifying our relation to our self and to our mode of existence. It is also made clear that this is an 'ethics of discomfort' or a form of 'ethical violence'.

Keywords Limit-attitude · Ethics · Self-formation · Genealogy · Critique

> I am not a writer, a philosopher, a great figure of intellectual life: I am a teacher (Foucault 1988c, p. 9)

> My role - and that is too emphatic a word - is to show people that they are much freer than they feel, that people accept as truth, as evidence, some themes which have been built up at a certain moment during history, and that this so-called evidence can be criticized and destroyed. To change something in the minds of people – that's the role of an intellectual. (Foucault 1988c, p. 9)

So I ask in this chapter—what can we learn from Foucault the teacher, the intellectual? How can we use Foucault to uneducate ourselves? What I answer is that we are invited to learn an attitude, a method, a relation to our own historicity, and our existence within and in relation to power. We are invited to learn the possibility of modifying our relation to our self and to our mode of existence. That is, to understand our constitution within power/knowledge, our fabrication; and thus we learn the limits of ourselves, and thus our revocability—the historical ontology of ourselves. This is an 'ethics of discomfort' or as Butler (2005) calls it a form of 'ethical violence'.

> To rebel against our educational present we must explore its perversions, its cynicisms. We should disabuse ourselves of our well-meaning but shallow commitments. To resist, we must become uncomfortable. This resistance will be an excoriating experience, where those who rebel feel ill at ease in their skin. (Allen 2014, p. 250)

© The Author(s) 2017
S.J. Ball, *Michel Foucault*, SpringerBriefs on Key Thinkers in Education,
DOI 10.1007/978-3-319-50302-8_2

What this rebellion involves is a destabilization, a challenge to everything that makes us what we are, without any of the comforts of another way of being—that 'other' remains 'undefined'. The point is that 'we must recognize that there is an outside, that we have limits, that we are finite' (Falzon 1998 p. 34). This is what Hook (2007, p. 3) calls a 'de-theorising project' aimed not at the construction of a grand theory of power but an analysis of its 'experiential force and logic' (ibid.). Nonetheless, in relation to this, we also learn the possibility of freedom, or perhaps the possibility of constructing a space to think about ways we might be free; we can also learn to struggle, we can learn how not to be governed that way, using the arts of 'voluntary insubordination' (see Chap. 3). This is modest yet momentous, in the sense that it requires us to question our own validity, to give up on essentialism and fixity and 'restore to things their mobility, their possibility of being modified' (Foucault 2016, p. 129).

This chapter will change emphasis from analytics to critique, from the apparent inevitability of domination, to the possibilities of deconstruction and troubling, and the next chapter takes this further by considering the practicalities of *self-formation*. Specifically in this chapter I will try to find my way among a set of relationships which animate and underpin some of Foucault's key intellectual tools: *critique, genealogy, the limit attitude, refusal, transgression and freedom*. In an interview given in the USA in 1980 Foucault outlines the three elements of what he calls his morals, which are a form of critical practice and an orientation to refusal and the possibility of being different.

> In a sense, I am a moralist, insofar as I believe that one of the tasks, one of the meanings of human existence—the source of human freedom—is never to accept anything as definitive, untouchable, obvious, or immobile. No aspect of reality should be allowed to become a definitive and inhuman law for us. (Foucault 1988b)

Fundamental to this task and the attitude in which it is grounded is an attempt to forge a different relation to power and to ourselves. The elements are '(1) the refusal to accept as self-evident the things that are proposed to us; (2) the need to analyse and to know, since we can accomplish nothing without reflection and understanding —thus, the principle of curiosity; and (3) the principle of innovation; to seek out in our reflection those things that have never been thought or imagined' (Ibid.). This highlights Hook's point that 'Foucault's most vital contribution … is less that of a theorist than that of a methodologist' (2007, p. 3)—methods of critique and methods of self-formation. Foucault offers not solutions, not transcendental or analytic verities, but practices.

The chapter will also consider genealogy and critique as an educational form, as a way of learning about how the world is made up, of understanding that things we take for granted have histories, of developing a sense that we might be other than who and what we seem. This is education as a form of politics. Following Butler (2006, p. 114), Youdell (2011, p. 28) points out that 'we might conceptualise the "cross cutting modalities of life" (Butler 1997), through which we are made meaningful to ourselves and to others and across which political struggles might be pursued'. Genealogy and critique also offer the potential for a re-politicisation of everyday life (Clarke 2012, p. 298), the re-opening to question of taken for granted and naturalised concepts, practices, relations and social arrangements. In education this might mean recognising the political force of issues like standards and accountability, ability, special educational needs, that are presented by pedagogues and policymakers in relation to practice, as matters of common sense or technical efficiency, foregrounding their disparity and power-effects, denaturalising the categories that organise and define our experience and make us what we are. Teaching and learning, the teacher and student, what it means to be educated are set into history, placed under doubt, subjected to sabotage and disruption. This takes us into a worrying, indeed frightening space in which we must 'un-think' education and recognise as fragile and contingent many of our modernist certainties—a space where knowledge is uncertain, truth is unstably linked to power, and our intelligibility is constantly in question.

Education and truth become de-coupled, indeed they become agonistic. We must accept that: 'Truth is a thing of this world: it is produced only by virtue of multiple forms of constraint. And it induces regular effects of power' (Foucault 1980b, p. 131). In one of the many re-renderings of his intellectual project, in the Preface to *The Use of Pleasure* (*The History of Sexuality Vol. 2*), Foucault describes his primary concern has having been focused on developing a 'history of truth'; with three main aspects. (1) An analysis of 'games of truth'—those systems of discourse that developed to produce truth. (2) The relation of these to power. (3) The relation of these to the self. This is another version of the three vectors (truth, power and subjectivity) discussed in Chap. 1. Gutting nicely contrasts Foucault's concern to put truth to the test with the 'unconditional love of truth' that is embedded in traditional philosophy (2005, p. 109) and we might add, traditional education. Foucault's orientation to truth is however developed somewhat different in his final body of work (see Chap. 3).

Critique

For Foucault then critique is an attitude or philosophical ethos and a form of engagement that combines outrage with limit-testing and careful scholarship. The point is to:

> criticise the working of institutions which appear to be both neutral and independent; to criticise them in such a manner that the political violence which has always exercised itself obscurely through them will be unmasked, so that one can fight them. (Foucault 1974, p. 171)

In other words, to criticise is to think about the ways in which current structures construct and constrain our possible modes of action and being. At its heart this is a curiosity towards the arts of being governed and thus the possibilities of refusal and innovation. However, the project of critique is not a particular and specific set of actions it is a permanent orientation of scepticism, it is 'a mode of relating to contemporary reality' (in Rabinow 1987, p. 39). In relation to this, Foucault studiously avoids the prescription of particular actions that should be employed in order to escape or oppose the phenomena of being governed. Instead, he asserts that criticism is comprised of 'analyzing and reflecting upon limits' (ibid., p. 45). It is 'the art of voluntary insubordination, and a practice of reflective intractibility' (ibid., p. 32).

> This philosophical ethos may be characterized as a limit-attitude. We are not talking about a
> gesture of rejection. We have to move beyond the outside-inside alternative; we have to be
> at the frontiers. (ibid., p. 45)

This is a form of liminal analysis, a stance of liminality that eshews modernist binaries and grand utopian gestures, and abstract formulations of freedom. Rather, Foucault writes of specific transformations in 'our ways of being and thinking, relations to authority, relations between the sexes, the way in which we perceive insanity or illness' (Foucault 1997c, p. 316). This requires 'the correlation of historical analysis and the practical attitude, to the programs for a new man that the worst political systems have repeated throughout the twentieth century'. This is not 'a theory, a doctrine' or the articulation of a body of knowledge, but 'the critique of what we are' and 'the historical analysis of the limits that are imposed on us and an experiment with the possibility of going beyond them' (Foucault 1997c, p. 306).

There is a duality here, as is often the case, Foucault took up a double, or paradoxical position in relation to the Enlightenment. On the one hand, drawing positively from Kant, the critical attitude, as a form of ethical practice is about our relation to ourself, and what we have become, as much as it is to something that is outside of ourselves. It is a form of disentanglement, a leverage of critique to open up opportunities for limit-testing. It is an attitude to the present which he termed a *philosophical ethos*. On the other hand, Foucault understands the Enlightenment as the age that paved the way for *the sciences of man* and the oppressions of rationality. That is, as discussed in the previous chapter, the sciences of discipline and normalization, of surveillance and control of bodies and souls, of marginalization and exclusion of the deviant, the abnormal, the insane. Here reason is not a neutral stance but rather 'a history of dogmatism and despotism a reason, consequently, which can only have an effect of emancipation on condition that it manages to liberate itself from itself [...] Reason as despotic enlightenment' (Rabinow 1987). In other words, he sought to radicalize Kant (Olssen 2003), to replace Kant's universalism with a principle of permanent contingency, to recognise the historically contingent character of all truth claims and thus make critique the 'historical investigation into the events that have led us to constitute ourselves and to recognize ourselves as subjects of what we are doing, thinking, saying' (Rabinow 1987, p. 46). Clearly, education is entangled in all of this, as a vehicle for reason and for its despotism; as a site of truth and its violence.

But let us back up a little here. How did we get here? We need to understand all of this as a new form of politics in relation to Foucault's conceptualization of truth, founded on his outline of a genealogy of power and articulated within some significant shifts over time in his thinking in relation to power. In introducing the

College de France lecture series of 1976—(Foucault 2004), he spoke, in his rather
disarming and disingenuous way, about changing direction and moving on from
what he described as 'making no progress' in his previous work, indeed he
described his work to that date as 'all leading nowhere. It's all repetitive, and it
doesn't add up ... Its all getting into something of an inextricable tangle'. From this
'inextricable tangle' he begins to outline a major move away from an emphasis on
power as domination to power as constitution. After *Discipline and Punish* there
appears to be a dual focus to his work with one aspect concerned with the
genealogy of the state and political rationalities (e.g. *The Birth of Biopolitics*, 2010)
and the other with the genealogy of the subject and concomitantly the problem of
ethics (e.g. *The Hermeneutics of the Subject*, 2005). These are connected up both
analytical and in a very practical way within the arts of government and specifically
those 'points of contact' between technologies of domination and technologies of
the self, forms of power and processes of *subjectification*. In general terms, the state
and the subject (in all the senses of the word) codetermine each other's emergence
(Lecture 8 February 1978).

> My general project over the past few years has been, to reverse the mode of analysis
> followed by the discourse of right from the time of the Middle Ages. With the aim,
> therefore to invert it, to give due weight, that is, to the fact of domination, to expose both its
> latent nature and its brutality. (Foucault 1980c)

There is, for Foucault, a concomitant refocusing of politics in relation to the
genealogy of power.

> Let us how things work at the level of on-going at the level of those continuous and
> uninterrupted processes which subject our bodies, govern our gestures, dictate our beha-
> viours etc. In other words, rather than ourselves how the sovereign appears to us in his lofty
> isolation, we should try to discover how it is that are gradually, really and materially
> through a multiplicity of organisms, forces, energies, desires, etc. (1980, p. 97)

What he argues in effect is that the politics of power has been focused in the
wrong place, on the wrong target, that is on the abstract state, rather than on the
flows of power invested in our everyday lives and immediate and intimate relations.
That is, rather than focus on power as having 'a single center' and 'general
mechanisms' or 'overall effects', if we want to understand power we should be
'looking at its extremities, at its outer limits at the point where it becomes capillary'
(Foucault 1982b, p. 27). This shift leads to a different materiality of power, to a
preoccupation with 'the bodies that are constituted as subjects by power-effects'
(Ibid., p. 29). Foucault's philosophical endeavour becomes reoriented to the
investigation of the modalities in which discourse and practices have turned human
beings into subjects of particular kinds (Marshall 1990).

Here then the individual is the site of power, the point at which it is enacted or
resisted/refused (Mills 2003) but never confronted in an absolute sense as some
external force, rather engaged within multiple 'strategic skirmishes' aimed at its
multiple points of application. The issue is one of recognising and unpicking the
multi-facetted and multifarious relations of power. Again, in respect to all of this,
Foucault uses key words with a dual meaning, the term *subject* has a two-fold

meaning, it is systematically ambiguous, both implying being tied 'to someone else by control or dependence', and to 'one's own identity by a conscience or self-knowledge' (1982, p. 212). The 'equivocal nature' of such terms, Foucault says, 'is one of the best aides in coming to terms with the specificity of power' (Foucault 1982a). The crucial point arising from all of is that subjectivity is the *point of contact*, a site of articulation, between self and power.

In this move in the conceptualization and history of power, Foucault sought to 'cut off the head of the king' (1979, p. 89) and following from this, as (Dean 1994b, p. 156) puts it, he asks 'How is it possible that this headless body behaves *as if* it indeed had a head'. The politics of all of this is that the conception of power is the basis for the struggle against it. This opens up a move beyond 'docile bodies'. Power is a generative mechanism but no particular manifestation of power is inevitable. Freedom concerns the will to exercise power differently. That is, the individual which power has constituted is at the same time its vehicle. To confront power we must address our relation to ourselves, and our immediate social relations. 'Everyone has their own Gulag, the Gulag is here at our door, in our cities, our hospitals, our prisons, its here in our heads' (Foucault 1977b). Walzer (1988, p. 199) captures this succinctly 'We must study the sites where power is physically administered and physically endured or resisted'. Foucault seeks to bring power closer to hand, close to home—which also makes it accessible, makes its limits visible, makes its refusal possible.

Thus, Foucault's critique is not simply of forms of power, but the politics of power, the conceptions, methods and practices of its contestation. In an interview in 1971, talking about his work with GIP (Groupe d'Information sur les Prisons),[1] he explained:

> the ultimate goal of [our] interventions was not to extend the visiting rights of prisoners to 30 min or to procure flush toilets for cells, but to question the social and moral distinction between the innocent and the guilty.

It is the code, the system, the knowleges and truth, the classifications on which the exercise of power is based that Foucault sets out to attack. Concomitantly, there is no independent position, no critical distance that enables us to develop abstract critical principles for this attack. This is not a matter of asserting a better alternative. And there is no natural or free subject to be liberated in this struggle. We are always the product of power relations, of codes and disciplines of some sort. There is no escape from power only the struggle against particular forms and manifestations of power. Again, as Walzer (1988, p. 202) says, 'he attacks the panoptic regime only because it is the regime under which he happens to live' and goes on to say: 'For him morality and politics go together' (p. 202). This is difficult to understand and easy to misunderstand. I will return to this later and in the following chapter.

---

[1]David Macey (1993, p. 262) referring to an interview Foucault gave in July 1971 says that he 'wanted to move away from abstraction. Particular circumstances and events had displaced his attention on to the prison problem. They also offered an escape from his boredom with "literary matters" ("la chose litteraire")'.

In some ways this is well-worked territory in terms of a radically different, and difficult, re-focusing of the analysis of power from will and might, the 'great machineries of power', to circulation and relations, from the sovereign and the state, to 'the delicate mechanisms of power' that are articulated in relation to apparatuses of knowledge and truth, from law to normalization, from the 'cognition-truth axis' to the 'discourse-power axis' (Foucault 2004, p. 178), from the Leviathan to 'techniques and tactics' of domination, the polymorphous mechanics of discipline—all of which is founded on a recognition that power itself has a history. But at the same time there is a clear sense of the heterogeneity of power, such that sovereignty and discipline can never be reduced 'one to the other' (ibid., p. 37). Indeed, Foucault suggests that discipline has colonized the procedures of the law, in such a way as to produce a 'normalizing society' (p. 39)—most specifically in the medicalisation or what other writers call the *biologisation* of society—biopolitics. Education plays a key role in the processes of biologisation, as Gulson and Webb (2016, p. xx) argue 'education policy also assumed the responsibilities of a molecular biopolitics that is part of imagining, legitimating, and constituting different forms of life'.

Foucault believed that we are more able to recognise power and its oppressions in the immediacy of our social relations than in the abstract politics of labour and capital. Critique is thus aimed at specific points of power, immediate institutional settings, and resistance is a set of provocations, mundane rebellions, without reference to pre-established moral positions or commitments, or even clear goals and purposes—rather 'an engagement with the numberless potential transgressions of those forces which war against our self-creation and solidarity' (Brenauer 1987). Walzer among many other critics (e.g. Bernstein 1992; Taylor 1989; Rorty 1986) is unconvinced by and unhappy with this. Walzer says finally of Foucault 'Angrily, he rattles the bars of the iron cage. But he has no plans or projects for turning the cage into something more like a human home' (1988 p. 209). But perhaps Walzer misjudges and misunderstands Foucault. He certainly fails to grasp that humanity is the cage, or one of the cages that Foucault seeks to rattle. The point is that humanity itself is something that makes us up—as 'man'. It is a productive limitation to what we might be. But also, over and against this, the possibilities of being freer than with think we are, the struggles that this opens up and their ethical substance are the basis for a creative and aesthetic politics, and not reliant on pre-given, tainted, moral principles that we take to define humanity. Thus, the erasure of 'man' that Foucault prophesises at the end of *The Order of Things* is not a 'deficiency' or a 'lacuna' but rather 'nothing more, and nothing less, than the unfolding of a space in which it is once more possible to think' (1970, p. 342). Drawing on Nietzsche Foucault is seeking to displace the humanist/progressive traditions of western philosophy, with their promise of personal well being and collective progress, and which require us to search for and link our essential qualities to inherent abstract principles, and instead to set the challenge 'of creatively and courageously authoring one's ethical self' (Pignatelli 2002, p. 158). The task is to avoid fixity in order to become a stylist, an ironist, a hero by 'tak[ing] oneself as object of a complex and difficult elaboration' (Foucault 1986, p. 166). Again, in a different way from the previous chapter, education as the transmission of knowledge and values and principles is thus made impossible—at least in the ways we have come to conceive of it as a canonical curriculum and an institutional practice.

However, Foucault was adamant that there is no simple relationship between critique and action. The focus, the problem for Foucault is the struggle against what is, and not, at least initially, to rush to delineate what might be an alternative. 'I think that to imagine another system is to extend our participation in the present system' (Foucault 1997b, p. 230). The primary task is as much one of refusal as it is resistance.

> The necessity of reform mustn't be allowed to become a form of blackmail serving to limit, reduce, or halt the exercise of criticism. Under no circumstances should one pay attention to those who tell one: "Don't criticize, since you're not capable of carrying out a reform." That's ministerial cabinet talk. Critique doesn't have to be the premise of a deduction that concludes, "this, then, is what needs to be done." It should be an instrument for those who fight, those who resist and refuse what is. (Rabinow and Rose 2003b, p. 84)

In other words, 'Foucault has invented a past for some future present' (Walzer 1988, p. 206) and rather than 'offer anaemic fore-closed readings of a possible future' (Pignatelli 2002, p. 158) we sift through the past 'in order to provide different and *distinct* ways of coming at our own problems and yearnings as ethical subjects' (p. 162). Rather than the enactment of a new (or old) set of principles or the creation of a systematic alternative social world, Foucault seems to be urging us to some kind of empirical experimentation (Foucault 1988a) within the space created by denunciation and the recognition that we might be different. This takes place not outside or beyond power but within some other kind of power relations, some kind of 'socialist art of government' (Defert and Ewald 2001, pp. 1155–1156), the absence of which Foucault thought had debilitated the political left in its failure to develop an 'autonomous governmentality' or as (Ferguson 2011, p. 67) suggests exercising power 'in a way that would be provisional, reversible, and open to surprise' an opportunistic polyvalence, a re-appropriation. For Foucault, as Miller (1993, p. 140) asserts, 'the world appears as a city to be built, rather than a cosmos already given'.

Of course for Foucault power is intimately entwined with knowledge, with systems of truth. Truth holds us under its thrall. As he says, nothing is true that is not the product of power. The concern here is not with *what is true*, but for Foucault, as with his other concerns, the *how* of truth and 'the system of truth and falsity' itself (Foucault 2013a). That is, how some things come to count as true. The political question … is not error, illusion … it is truth itself (Foucault 1980a, p. 133). So that 'instead of trying to find out what truth' we would be better advised to try to understand why we accord traditionally conceived truth ultimate value. Truth is 'a system of constraint which is exercised not only on other discourses, but on a whole series of other practices' (Foucault 2013b, p. 2). These discourses and practices 'present themselves to subjects as environments fully on a par with the physical environment' (Prado 2006). As Youdell (2006, p. 35) explains such discourses are 'located and real and constrained—make some things possible, or even likely, and others all but impossible'. There is a silent coupling of knowledge and power as a means by which we assign people to positions/categories and assign them value/worth. For example 'the promise that categorization and comparison through standardised measurements will reveal and illuminate essential truths about students, teachers and schools' (Pignatelli 1993). Thus, Burchell (1996) argues that a genealogist, an historian of the present must always 'have a concern for truth' (p. 31) and 'must be meticulous in describing the shapes it assumes' (p. 32). This means that we must address the 'general politics of truth' within our neoliberal society and 'the types of discourse which it accepts and makes function as true' (Foucault 1980, p. 131). And, of course, the value and effectivity of truth rests on the status of those enabled and designated to produce and speak and apply it to others, those whom in the present Rose (1996, p. 54) calls the *grey scientists*. The point of critique and the work of genealogy is not to produce an account that is more truthful or closer to the truth but to sabotage and disrupt validity and meaning by exposing the conditions for the formation of truth and to undermine its incumbents; as Foucault asserts 'knowledge is not made for understanding; it is made for cutting' (Foucault 1977a, p. 154).

In the enactment of judgement and the practices of evaluation and comparison, truth[2] thus articulates our 'discursive currency' (Prado 2006, p. 80). That is, ways of thinking and talking about ourselves, to ourselves and to others—'a regime of truth offers the terms that make self-recognition possible' (Butler 2005, p. 22). This is a form of violence that acts upon our relation to ourselves, our self-recognition and our subjectivity—one form of this, about which I have written, is performativity (Ball 2003).

The subject under the regime of performativity is made calculable rather than memorable, malleable rather than committed, flexible rather than principled, productive rather than ethical. Experience is nothing, productivity is everything, comparisons and judgments, and the multiple ways in which we *account* for ouselves makes us transparent and accountable—depthless. Social relations are replaced by informational structures. We are made responsible for our performance and for the performance of others. Within the contemporary technocratic market regime of neoliberalism the relationships of truth and power are articulated and operationalized more and more in terms of forms of performance, or outputs, and expressed in the reductive form of numbers. This is the 'numericisation of politics' as Legg (2005 p. 143) calls it. In the lecture series *Security, Territory, Population* (2009), Foucault explores how the emerging European states began to deal with the disease of smallpox from the eighteenth century onwards. Rather than deploying techniques of exclusion or quarantine, as for leprosy and the plague, the focus for medical intervention rested on determining probabilities and establishing averages through the use of statistics. That is, 'knowing how many people were infected with smallpox, at what age, with what effects, with what mortality rate, lesions or

---

[2]Foucault does not offer a definition of truth; rather he provides a multi-faceted characterization (Prado 2006, p. 81).

after-effects, the risks of inoculation, the probability of an individual dying or being infected by smallpox despite inoculation, and the statistical effects on the population in general' (2009, p, 10), In this way, 'the technology of statistics creates the capacity to relate to reality as a field of government' (Hunter 1996, p. 154) both in the management of individuals and of the population. Indeed, 'Population is a concept that can be elaborated only through statistical, therefore informational techniques' (Koopman 2014, p. 102) or as Foucault (2009, p. 79) suggests, there is 'a constant interplay between techniques of power and their object gradually carves out in reality, as a field of reality, population and its specific phenomena. A whole series of objects were made visible for possible forms of knowledge…'.

This interplay, this making visible, and the concomitant possibilities for government are all very evident now both, on the one hand, in the generation of big-data (see Chideya 2015) and, on the other, in local applications of measurement, for example in what Bradbury (2013) calls the *datafication* of the pre-school classroom. An extract from one of my MA student essays illustrates this very nicely.

> Schools are littered with data; at times it seems that everything I do as a practitioner is valued only in as far as it impacts positively on the data. Schools are fashioned by external forces acting upon the practitioners desire to do the right thing. What is achieved is summed up in a series of charts, graphs, tables and detailed statistical analysis. The value we place on everything we do is formed by its relationship to the measure.

Cracking the Grid

To illustrate further the operation and effectivity and interplay of truth, power and subjectivity as performativity, and the struggle against these truths, I want to draw upon the experiences and voices of a group of teachers with whom I have been in email contact over a number of years. These are teachers who found aspects of their experience of school 'cracked' and grating, discomforting and untenable. They have been seeking ways of understanding and challenging the contemporary, over-bearing truths of measurement and comparison, and ways of representing themselves and their practice differently. Raymond, one teacher correspondent wrote:

> My first introduction to 'accountability' was a talk with a head teacher which kind of finally burst the bubble and destroyed any romantic ideal I had that teaching was an art and honorable profession. It became very much the numbers game and I had to sail close to my moral and ethical boundaries to do well.

The regime of numbers hails us in its terms, and to the extent we turn, acknowledge and engage, we are made recognizable and subject. Once in its thrall we are reduced by it to a category or quotient—our worth, our humanity and complexity are abridged. However, as Butler suggests, when we 'question the regime of truth', we also question also our 'own ontological status' (Butler 2005), an issue I return to later. The question is what kind of self, what kind of subject have we become, and how might we be otherwise? Or more succinctly: 'Maybe the target nowadays is not to discover what we are but to refuse what we are.' (Foucault 1982a, p. 785) and perhaps 'refusing, changing and ridding ourselves are only the ethical conditions, made possible by genealogical work, of creation, innovation and invention' (Cremonesi 2013, p. 14). This is one form of what Foucault called in his Dartmouth Lectures (2013, p. 15) a 'politics of ourselves'. That is to say, 'All those on whom power is exercised to their detriment, all who find it intolerable, can begin the struggle on their own terrain and on the basis of their proper activity (or passivity)' (Deleuze and Foucault 1977, p. 216). Let me quote from another of the teachers with whom I have been exchanging emails. Nigel, a Primary school headteacher:

> I am a victim of the 'terrors of performativity'. The notion of calibrating performance sets in stone what is to be measured and how, and also gives power to a cadre, who are handed the status of determinators. Hubris takes over, just as so too interpretative awareness and social insight implode. We also have associate assessors, but because our inspections system is about matching to a grade I wouldn't touch it with a barge pole (…) That is the space I operated in. It was never about imposing a judgement. My thinking has slowly shifted, through reading and contacts such as with you. Also by developments of practice, and making links with those developing techniques or materials. I have found others immensely influencing of my own professional growth: Pasi Sahlberg, John Macbeath, Andy Hargreaves, Dennis Shirley, Joe Bower, Maurice Holt, Carol Fitz-gibbon. But that is a character set who don't fit the performativity mould. (Nigel).

What this illustrates I think is the will to struggle against the anonymity of power and its 'dispersed and discontinuous offensives' (Foucault 1988c)—its practices and its truths and their effects and outcomes. In this instance Nigel has other discursive resources through which he can strive to articulate himself differently over and against the 'determinations' and celebrations of measurement. Nonetheless, the prevailing 'discursive currency' of neoliberal education is also made clear by Martin, another correspondent, a US school Principal.

> I find that one of the most fundamental challenges of my job is trying to avoid becoming incorporated into market modes of thinking. Of course, the more time you spend at work trying to please your superiors, the more you use the language of performativity and begin to believe in it yourself. And then, when I go back to my dissertation, it is difficult to be surprised by the data.

Martin is also here, I think, articulating a sense that he might be recognisable differently, might think about himself differently, and those possibilities rest on a realisation of what he has become what he does not want to be—that is enabled in part by his dissertation work, a form of critique and work on himself, which I will come back to.

Genealogy

As indicated above, one technique and form of struggle against the violence of representation for those who seek to challenge the limits of our possibility, the necessity of things, the inevitability of experience, is genealogy.

> Hard and patient labour of detailed historical and empirical work, as necessary to question and reformulate presumed continuities and discontinuities, so that it is possible to offer diagnoses of the limits and possibilities of the present. (Dean 2010, pp. 57–58)

Genealogy is a form of historical practice that Foucault borrowed from Nietzsche's *Genealogy of Morals*, but made his own.

> The only valid tribute to a thought such as Nietzsche's is precisely to use it, to deform it, to make it groan and protest. And if commentators then say that I am being faithful or unfaithful to Nietzsche, that is of absolutely no importance. (Foucault 1980a, pp. 53–54)

Foucault's genealogies always begin from his perception that something is terribly wrong in the present. That something is 'intolerable'. Genealogy seeks to trace and challenge the origins of practices and institutions from congeries of contingent 'petty causes' through the elaboration of professional expertise and erudite knowledge—the knowledge of types, classes, categories and cases—the tyranny of the intellect, rationales of subjection. It is a strategy for mapping out the topology of local situations. Such histories replace inevitability with contingency, and hence construct the suppressibility of what history has given us. It does this in part by revalidating excluded or marginalized voices, like those of the teachers quoted above, and re-articulating different forms of self-recognition and veridiction that are otherwise 'buried or masked in functional coherences or formal systematisations' (Foucault 2004, p. 7). This is both an 'insurrection of subjugated knowledges' (p. 7) and a local and 'theoretically modest' practice (Blacker 1998, p. 357).

> It is the relation of the genealogist to her own contemporaneity; the realisation of the genealogist's position as a trace within her own analysis and the further realisation that this trace has an effect on the present, that is, on the local struggles of the genealogist's situation. (Mackenzie 1994)

Genealogies produce a form of *ethopoietic knowledge*, knowledge that works to modify our way of being our mode of existence (Foucault 2005, p. 237). The point 'is not to discover a ... positive foundation of the self ... [but] that the self is nothing else than the historical correlation of the technology built in our history'— that is the 'link between political work and historical inquiry' (Foucault 2016, p. 91), the work of making things more fragile, without recourse to what Foucault called *anthropologism*, to an essential human and an essential humanism.

> genealogy is, then, a sort of attempt to desubjugate historical knowledges, to set them free, or in other words to enable them to oppose and struggle against the coercion of a unitary, formal, and scientific theoretical discourse. The project of these disorderly and tattered genealogies is to reactivate local knowledges.... (2004, p. 10).

Genealogy is neither systematic nor precise, and Foucault's accounts of the method are not consistent to say the least. It is rather an orientation to history and its specific address is to the claims to cognitive authority made by specific disciplines—like penality and psychiatry and as I have suggested in the previous chapter, pedagogy, and in a different way performativity.[3] A genealogy is an attempt to consider the origins of systems of knowledge, and to analyze the centralising power-effects of discourses. 'Genealogy has to fight the power-effects characteristic of any discourse that is regarded as scientific' (Foucault 2004, p. 9). In effect, genealogies are 'anti-sciences' (ibid., p. 9). They attempt to reveal the discontinuities and breaks in a discourse, to focus on the specific rather than on the general. In doing so, they aim to show that there have been other ways of thinking and acting, and that modern discourses are not any truer than those in the past. They are about 'how to make the unfamiliar familiar, to show that the past is not so different from today in certain respects' (Dean 2010, p. 57). As Dreyfus and Rabinow explain it:

> Genealogy accepts the fact that we are nothing but our history, and that therefore we will never get a total and detached picture either of who we are or of our history…we must inevitably read our history in terms of our current practices. (Dreyfus and Rabinow 1983)

Things 'can be unmade as long as we know how it was they were made' (Foucault quoted in Ransom (1997, p. 89). Foucault's point is that we must not take for granted the relations entwining power and knowledge but rather that those relations need to be explored in every case. Furthermore, as suggested above, to grasp the reach and force of Foucault's project the *subject* needs to be inserted between power/knowledge. That is to say, power relations are always instantiated in certain 'fields of knowledge, types of normativity and forms of subjectivity' (Foucault 1992, p. 4). Experts, grey scientists, and their knowledges, their truths, play a key role in determining how we should act and who we are, operationalized within material practices—the confession, the annual review, inspections, 360° evaluations etc.

Genealogy is the method for addressing 'cases'. Doing genealogies means avoiding the search for depth, and rather having a focus on the superficial, that is on details, on the nitty-gritty, but certainly not the trivial. This is a primary focus on practices rather than laws, on discourses rather than rhetorics, on techniques and procedures and architectures rather than social structures. By exposing these to scrutiny, the intention is to make things not as necessary as all that, to make them 'human, all too human'. It is 'from the contingency that has made us what we are' that comes 'the possibility of no longer being, doing, or thinking what we are to do, or think' (Foucault 1997c, p. 316). This is Foucault's 'epistemology of suspicion' (Scott-Baumann 2009). Genealogies are histories that focus on the interplay of knowledge and power, and seek to destabilize nature and the self, and undermine claims to authority, making them problematic, difficult and dangerous. They address

---

[3]In as much that the techniques of performativity are increasing formalized within a disciplinary framework, a scientistic basis for the practice of measurement.

'practical issues, necessities, and the limits of the present' (Dean 1994a, p. 20) starting from 'questions posed in the present' (Foucault 1998, p. 262). 'This has massive implications for education' Youdell (2006, p. 36) argues 'because it insists that nobody is necessarily anything and so what it means to be a teacher, a student, a learner might be opened up to radical rethinking'.

The prison, for Foucault, served as a paradigmatic site for an exploration of the relations between contemporary discourses and practices, as a symbolic form, an inverted image of society.[4] *Discipline and Punish* is intended 'to recover the theme of the genealogy of morals' and trace changes in the 'moral technologies' that constitute the mundane practices of punishment—that is 'places where what is said and what is done, rules imposed and reasons given, the planned and taken for granted meet and interconnect' (quoted in Mahon 1992, pp. 130–131). From his analysis of prisons Foucault discerns a specific 'modern' form of power—discipline —which functions to produce, transform or make modern individuals and to normalise behaviour; 'it is a modest, suspicious power, which functions as a calculated, but permanent economy' (Foucault 1980a, pp. 124–125) or as Osborne (2009, p. 133) asserts 'what is described takes the form not of something elevated and transhistorical, but something lowly, worldly and tied to the exigencies of power'.

Given all of this, if we return to the question of what we can learn from Foucault, MacIntyre (1990) argues that he leaves us trapped in a damaging paradox. Indeed he suggests that genealogy is self-defeating and impossible—that it undermines and vitiates its own claims. He argues that the lecturer who espouses the genealogical method, eliminates at the same time their own authority, their own claims.

> From the genealogical standpoint what is needed is some way of enabling the members of the audience to regard themselves from an ironic distance and, in so separating themselves from themselves, to open up the possibility of an awareness of these fissures within the self … And among the purposes to be served by both theatre and genealogical commentary will be the undermining of all traditional forms of authority, including the authority of the lecturer. MacIntrye (1990) (quoted in Osborne 2009, p. 130).

A retort to this might be that this is an authority that Foucault has already abdicated, in part in his claims to write only fictions. The audience is not asked to regard the claims of the genealogist as superior to those claims made by other 'scientists' but to treat all and any claims to truth with irony and scepticism—to take on the critical attitude. The stance and response required from the audience is not one of affirmation but the cultivation of an ironic detachment towards the present and a recognition that their selfhood has a history (see Chap. 3). Osborne (2009, p. 130) argues that what is at stake here is not 'research of an orthodox, positive or 'scientific sort', indeed in part at least these fictions are aesthetic[5]—they

---

[4]He made a visit to Attica prison in 1972.

[5]See Goldstein (1994). Introduction. In J. Goldstein (Ed.), *Foucault and the Writing of History*. Oxford: Blackwell. For discussion of Foucault's fascination with writing and literary aesthetics.

do not attempt to submit themselves to the procedures of the human sciences'. Indeed (MacKenzie 1994) suggests that their role is one of catharsis. Foucault he says:

> exposes the limits of his thought in order that these limits may be diffused. This is the reflexive moment, the moment where Foucault recognises his works as "fictions", the moment, the movement, of the fold of thought back on itself … This is the cathartic function of self-critical thought.

Transgression

Foucault offers genealogy as a diagnostic then, a historical method that enables history to 'become a curative science' by dismantling the teleological narratives that inscribe the subject as sovereign, and power as 'a phenomenon of mass and homogeneous domination' (2003, p. 29). The task of the genealogy here is to encourage the kind of: 'dissociating view that is capable of decomposing itself, capable of shattering the unity of man's being through which he could extend his sovereignty to events of the past. To dismantle belief in eternal truth the immortality of the soul and the nature of consciousness as always identical to itself' (Rabinow 1987, p. 87) and so facilitate another kind of history.

This is what Foucault calls effective history; that is, '…the reversal of a relationship of forces, the usurpation of power, the appropriation of a vocabulary turned against those who had once used it, a feeble domination that poisons itself as it grows lax, the entry of a masked "other"' (Foucault 1977a, p. 154). This is a history that works to deprive the self of the reassuring stability of life and nature. It is the means by which we are able to dismantle 'the comprehensive view of history as a patient and continuous development' (ibid., p. 160). It is an alternative to the enlightenment story of rational progress in which rationality is seen as constituting its opposite, as a form of tyranny that makes possible and necessary the confinement, medicalization and normalisation, the education or re-education, of those deemed abnormal or dangerous. However Foucault goes on to argue that critique is not 'a gesture of rejection […] the critical question today has to be turned back into a Positive one […] the point, in brief, is to transform the critique conducted in the form of necessary limitation into a practical critique that takes the form of a possible transgression' (Rabinow 1987, p. 54).

This is a problematizing, transgressive style of thinking oriented toward challenging existing ways of being and doing, with a view to liberating new possibilities for advancing 'the undefined work of freedom'. A 'limit-attitude' is a particular orientation towards discursive categories and institutional formations. In tracing the edges or outer contours of systems of thought Foucault raises the possibility of transgressing these in order to expose and disrupt the underlying relations between knowledge and power and thus the formation of subjects. 'In this sense, critique aims to free us from the historically transitory constraints of contemporary consciousness as realised in and through discursive practices' (Olssen 2003, p. 1).

We are incited to transgress normal thinking and to abandon the conceptual structures upon which such thinking draws and look beyond them, to make rationality unreasonable, to think beyond or outside the common-sense of the present—'to stand detached from it, bracketing its familiarity, in order to analyse the theoretical and practical context with which it has been associated' (Foucault 1992, p. 3). This means taking limits very seriously, on the one hand realising their necessity and productivity, but on the other recognizing that this necessity is historical and hence can be transcended.

Critique is a form of 'limit attitude', 'a means by which a subject can positively resist power through testing the limits of domination and subjection' (Hartmann 2003, p. 11), through 'counter-conducts', creative strategies of resistance that 'open up processes of 'autonomous and independent' subjectivation, that is, possibilities for the constitution of oneself' (Lazzarato 2009, p. 114). Counter-conducts are 'struggle[s] against processes implemented for conducting others' and begin with an explicit acknowledgement that efforts at government are not always successful, inciting as they do instances of 'resistance, refusal or revolt' (Foucault 2009, p. 266). Davidson (2001, p. 37) characterises such resistance as 'an active intervention… in the domain of the ethical'. That is, a refusal to be governed 'this way', a resistance to practices, a rejection of the discourses that animate the norms of political conduct, but it is not 'outside' or over and against power in any simple way. Power and resistance are mutually constitutive (see Davidson 2001).

Mackenzie (1994) argues that: 'It is a commonplace among commentators on Foucault's work that his thought is aimed at provoking a "limit-attitude" towards discursive categories and institutional formations' and he cites O'Farrell (1989) and Lemert and Gillan (1982). He goes on to argue that 'This interpretation of the Foucauldian project, however, is more useful as a starting point than as an end point; it is a place to begin critical discussion of his work not a way of summing it up'. The problem here is exactly a version of Foucault's method and his critique. Many of his critics, as noted above, seek to import or search for some kind of normative basis for criticism, some kind of foundational thinking. So, Hartmann (2003) asks whether the 'contestation of specific objects and impositions of power'—are entirely reactive? McCarthy (1994) suggests that it is difficult to identify 'just what it is that resists'. Rather as suggested previously Foucault's conception of transgression is at once a practice (of freedom) and a kind of liminality—creating the possibility of something different, of something unthought, rather than predicting it. But at the same time there must be an acceptance that what is important is the attempt, the struggle. Freedom is not an end point or a set of principles, it is a state of being, a mode of life.

> I mean that this work done at the limits of ourselves must, on the one hand, open up a realm of historical inquiry, and on the other, put itself to the test of reality, of contemporary reality, both to grasp the points where change is possible and desirable, and to determine the precise form this change should take. This means that the historical ontology of ourselves must turn away from all projects that claim to be global or radical. In fact we know from experience that the claim to escape from the system of contemporary reality…has led to the return of the most dangerous traditions. (Rabinow 1987)

Foucault is quite aware that this liberating criticism, this work done 'at the limits of ourselves', must be experimental, so that it may be able 'both to grasp the points where change is possible and desirable, and to determine the precise form this change should take' (Rabinow 1987, p. 46). At the same time criticism must also give up the hope of ever acceding 'to any complete and definitive knowledge of what may constitute our historical limits' (ibid., p. 47). Mackenzie (1994) puts this very bleakly: 'The hope that there may be a residual humanism that binds human beings in some moral community is also a futile hope, the modern subject is a fabrication of the times and constituted through the operation of multiple applications of power'.

The identification and criticism of limits and the possibility of moving beyond them are always limited; but rather than being a drawback, we should acknowledge that this is what enables us to always begin again. Criticism, in other words, must be constantly reactivated: only in this way can it provide an impetus to our 'undefined work of freedom'. Indeed, 'In Foucault a theory of the liminal is "brash" in its silence' (MacKenzie 1994). Criticism and limit-testing of this kind have an immediacy in their connection with people's lives. They do not call-up and rely on prior principles produced elsewhere, but are formed and forged in relation to 'concrete questions, difficult cases, revolutionary movements, reflections and evidence … It is all a social enterprise' (Foucault 1991). That is, a political enterprise as much as it is an epistemic one, an everyday politics of disruption and redefinition which speaks possibilities within silence. Foucault's intention was to 'learn to what extent the effort to think one's own history can free thought from what it silently thinks, and so enable it to think differently' (1992, p. 9)—a series is articulated: that is, critique—intolerance—self formation. Genealogical knowledge here is not informative it is transformative. To enable us to escape the intimacy of our experience within which power is naturalised, and freedom subordinated to reason. However, Osborne (2009, p. 135) warns us to take care with the notion of critique in relation to Foucault's practice and method of history, which consists not simply of 'the pious un-masking of the critic but, ultimately, the humorous stare of genealogist'.

As Allen (2014, p. 30) suggests 'transgression emerged in Foucault's writing as a subversive tactic which could enable individuals to transform themselves' and goes on to explain that transgression 'works at the limits that have defined ways of being, doing, and thinking, seeking the ever present possibility of the 'undefined work of freedom' (Dean 1994a). That is 'looking for what has not yet been thought, imagined or known' (Foucault 1980/2013, p. 128). All of this rests on the effort of what Blacker (1998, p. 360) calls 'attentiveness' 'to how one's actions get absorbed by the power/knowledge regime', or what Maxine Greene calls *wideawakeness*.

Human beings define themselves through the projects with which they become involved. By means of engagement with a project, the attitude of wide-awakeness develops and contributes to the choice of actions that lead to self-formation.

(http://www.newfoundations.com/GALLERY/Greene.html).

This then is a *negative* ethics—and ethics of avoidance, based upon renunciation, exile,[6] homelessness, disengagement, and a dispersion of the 'serene unity of subjectivity'—not a search for positive values or for alternatives. Nonetheless, this can open up new horizons for experiments in democracy and human relationships (Foucault 1997a), explorations in collective refusal perhaps. Here discipline and self-government are turned back on themselves as a freedom of possibilities rather than abstract illusions. Although (Ross 2008) suggests the politics of 'self stylisation' perhaps has limited aspirational force, and she again relates this to Foucault's 'considered refusal of the tendency to overestimate possible counter-paths'.

All of this begs questions in relation to education and what it means to be educated to which I will return in the next chapter. In particular it raises questions about what lies beyond critique; what are the goals or end points of transgression?

Also all of this is highly unsettling and disconcerting, the coherence of the subject, or rather the 'matrix of intelligibility' (Ross 2008), which underwrites the subject, is threatened. For Butler, a genealogy is 'an enquiry into the conditions of emergence of what is called history, a moment of emergence that is not finally distinguishable from fabrication' (Butler 1990, p. 15). It is about the processes and discourses through which someone is subjectivised and the history of things—like sentiments, conscience, instinct—that do not have histories. We are ourselves at risk in this enterprise, we make our being and experience contingent.[7] Telling the truth about oneself comes at a price: 'the price of that telling is the suspension of a critical relation to the truth regime in which one lives' (ibid., p. 122). Butler explains how Foucault 'would locate the practices of the subject as one site where those social conditions are worked and reworked' (p. 133). In other words, the subject is engaged in an ongoing struggle between a critical relation to the truth regime within which one lives and giving a 'truthful' account of the self. For this reason, Butler urges us 'to risk ourselves' and to be willing 'to become undone by another' (ibid., p. 136). 'If we speak and try to give an account from this place,' she argues, 'we will not be irresponsible, or, if we are, we will surely be forgiven' (p. 136). This is an 'ethic of discomfort,' that is, an ethic which embraces discomfort as a point of departure for individual and social transformation (Butler 1999), indeed 'some discomfort is not only unavoidable but may also be necessary' (p. 164). Foucault defines an ethic of discomfort as:

> never to consent to being completely comfortable with one's own presuppositions. Never to let them fall peacefully asleep, but also never to believe that a new fact will suffice to overturn them; never to imagine that one can change them like arbitrary axioms, remembering that in order to give them the necessary mobility one must have a distant view, but also look at what is nearby and all around oneself. To be very mindful that everything one perceives is evident only against a familiar and little known horizon, that every certainty is sure only through the support of a ground that is always unexplored. The most fragile

---

[6]See the risks of truth-telling in Chap. 3.

[7]Perhaps here we see some dim and hazy relations to Foucault's interest in neoliberalism. But this is not the same thing as becoming a neoliberal.

instant has its roots. In that lesson, there is a whole ethic of sleepless evidence that does not rule out, far from it, a rigorous economy of the True and the False; but that is not the whole story. (Zembylas 2015, p. 166)

As Zembylas (2015, p. 166) goes on to explain, Foucault's intention is to problematize manifestations of discomfort 'without portraying them as acts of bad faith or cowardice, to open a space for movement without slipping into a prophetic posture'. There is no retreat here to either a unitary or *essential* subject—'... it is already one of the prime effects of power that certain bodies, certain gestures, certain discourses, certain desires, come to be identified and constituted as individuals...the individual is an effect of power' (Foucault 1980, p. 98). Indeed, this may instigate what De Lissovoy (2010) calls 'the crisis of the subject' which he sees as a stage 'in a dynamic process ... rather than a simple switch in point of view or affiliation'. Established and perhaps cherished professional skills and judgements are made unreliable[8] in this process. As Blacker (1998) cogently argues we should not expect the consistency of a tightly integrated social subject, for that is part of what must be given up. Neither does this analysis mean that the configuration of struggle is, nor are its starting points, always the same. In various sites we may need help, from our Unions, colleagues, political allies, friends and family etc. 'Alliances of shifting points of resistance around concentrations of power become a possibility' (Rabinow and Rose 2003a, p. xxvii). Tactics will vary between sites and issues and the conditions of possibility also vary. The 'question concerns ways to mobilize, focus or intensify practices of resistance, in so far as they are already all over the place' (Macleod and Durrheim 2002). Refusal is everywhere in the field of everyday life, but there is 'no single locus of great Refusal, no soul of revolt' (Foucault 1981, p. 96) but rather shifting points of resistance that 'inflame certain parts of the body, certain moments in life' (Foucault 1981, p. 96). Transgression may take different forms and there are 'numberless potential transgressions' (Nealon 2008, p. 105). Transgression is strategic, made up of small acts and short-lived incursions that make limits visible and breachable, that unsettle convention, that deploy irony, that sketch out new possibilities which may be over-written and re-drawn. As Bernauer (1987, p. 139) notes, 'parodic displacement ... depends on a context and reception in which subversive confusions can be fostered' At the same time we have to accept that 'resistance is never in a position of exteriority in relation to power' (Butler 1990, p. 95). Resistance is not outside or over and against power but 'in' a relation to it, in a relation to practices. There is always the danger of incorporation and relations of power and resistance are unpredictable (ibid., p. 96).

In relation to all of this I have tried to argue (Foucault 1981) that in neoliberal economies, sites of government and *points of contact*, are also sites for the possibility of refusal. The starting point for a politics of refusal is the site of subjectivity.

---

[8]Perhaps this is something like Du Bois' (1905/1995) idea of *double consciousness*, a form of living between a damaged oppressed self and a sense of who you might want to be, beyond oppression.

It is a struggle over and against what it is we have become and what it is that we do not want to be. That is, a modern form of politics for a modern form of government. Struggle on this terrain is an engagement with and can involve *a refusal of neoliberal governmentality in its own terms*. '… there is no first or final point of resistance to political power than in the relation one has to oneself' (Foucault 1981, p. 252). In effect what Foucault does, in refusing to pander to our modern enlightenment political sensibilities, is to leave us, as ethical subjects with the discomforts and task of finding a way forward that is beyond common sense, outside of the limits of our imagination and the impossibility of speaking 'of anything which goes beyond its categories, and because there is no 'outside', we are unable to give any kind of explanation of the categories or terms through which we comprehend the world' (Falzon 1998, p. 31). Falzon goes on to argue that what is needed here is not self-negation, but an 'encounter between ourselves and the other' (p. 39)—a dialogue. A dialogue founded on creative activity and on transgression as 'the permanent possibility of the irruption of the other, the new and unexpected, at the margins of our existence' (ibid., p. 56)

> if power functions through the structuration of a field of possible actions, resistance to power should not only be understood in terms of agonistic power relations, but in terms of a creative traversing of the field of possible action. Resistance – positive resistance – is no longer merely reversal, but consists in a subject's becoming-autonomous within a structured set of institutions and practices through immanent critique (Hartmann 2003 p. 10).

This is what Falzon calls 'the fundamental encounter with the other' (1998, p. 36) not as a conceptual exercise but 'also as a concrete, palpable experience' (p. 33), within which 'our narcissistic reveries are shattered, the circle of our solipsism is burst' (p. 34).

Butler (2006, p. 114) is one writer/activist who follows this line of thought, she takes up Foucault and takes him in a different directions—appropriately deforming him, as he did Nietschze—and with a particular concern with gender, which she addresses from Foucault's anti-essentialist view of the body and sexuality and the ways in which deployments of power are directly connected to the body, historically and biologically—how the female is made feminine. According to Butler, material structures are sedimented through ritualised repetitions of conduct by embodied agents. In addressing refusal and resistance Butler writes of the need for *re-description* and of 'the act and strategy of disavowal' (1998, p. 530) that is not some kind of utopianism but 'an imperative to acknowledge the existing complexity of gender which our vocabulary invariably disguises' (Butler 1998). This is done perhaps in ways which mute some aspects of Foucault's 'politics of ourselves', Butler writes of the need to oppose, refuse, to subvert the language that renders us subject, in creative and dis-arming ways. Butler also talks about this as *resignification*, a linguistic reformulation of the notion of genealogical reinterpretation. As she says elsewhere "the possibility of resignification [is that of] mobilising… what Nietzsche, in *On the Genealogy of Morals*, called the 'sign chain'" (Butler 1998, p. 530). The *resignification* of a term alters and redirects the meaning sedimented within that term through pre-existing relationships, and beyond this she writes of 'subversive resignification'. These are embodied re-enactments of norms in ways that undermine the meanings traditionally entrenched within them. *Subversive resignifications* do this by *openly displaying* their status as re-enactments of norms. Butler (1997, p. 135) argues, qua Foucault, that the norms that constitute us are unstable and so constantly 'open to resignification, redeployment, subversive citation from within'. Thus, she suggests, the permanent instability of signs makes agency possible, in the form of the capacity to resignify norms that is 'through radical acts of public misappropriation such that the conventional relation between [interpellation and meaning] might become tenuous and even broken over time' (Butler 1997, p. 100). This brings together a form of critique with transgression and 'voluntary insubordination', founded on outrage and a 'limit attitude', testing and transgressing the limits of language and intelligibility, with an appropriate dose of irony and humour. Such a 'performative politics' Butler asserts offers 'an unanticipated political future for deconstructive thinking' (1997, p. 161) and are designed to expose hegemonic conceptions of identity as fictions.

Like Foucault, Butler has been subject to the criticism that her politics of resignification is irredeemably individualistic. For example, from a neo-Marxist perspective, (Boucher 1995, p. 114) argues that 'Having located the basis for resistance in individual psychology, Butler conceptualises this resistance in phenomenological terms of personal narratives and subjective melancholy, in abstraction from structural determinants such as material interests or crisis tendencies of the social system'. However, as Youdell (2006, p. 35) explains, while 'post-structural ideas have been charged with relativism, self-indulgence, an evacuation of politics' such criticisms 'miss the crucial point that the practice of deconstruction is itself a political practice' that can 'help us to understand and unsettle the relationship between the subject, the institution, power and meaning' as is 'critical to politically engaged scholarship and action in education' (pp. 40–1).

At the heart of transgression is a practice of agonism, the attempt to wrest self-formation from the techniques of government and to make oneself intelligible in different but unanticipated terms. The attempt—local and immediate—to conduct oneself differently, to forge an aesthetics of being, and to loosen the connection between subjectification and subjection. That is, not a going back, not a search for something repressed, but a going beyond that involves experiments with limits and possibilities—thinking about what one is now and how one *might* be different. In other words, this is the *care of the self*, the work of the 'politics of the self', a continuous practice of introspection, which is at the same time attuned to a critique of the world outside: 'critique is the movement through which the subject gives itself the right to question truth concerning its power effects and to question power about its discourses of truth. Critique will be the art of voluntary inservitude, of reflective indocility' (Foucault 1997c, p. 388). As Foucault (1997b) puts it, very straightforwardly: 'agency lies in the constant interplay between strategies of power and resistance'. (I shall return to this and to the role of subjugated knowledge in the next chapter).

What is at stake is how we are constituted and how we recognise ourselves through technologies—the intellectual, practical instruments and devices which shape and guide 'being human', or more specifically here, being a teacher or a researcher. That is, the activity of the subject within a field of constraints, crafting or re-crafting one's relation to oneself and to others or 'local problems, local solutions' (Mayo 2007). This is, 'ongoing, localised, contextually sensitive—but potentially generalised—practices about educational equity, practices that may well, indeed must, trouble our thinking about education' (Youdell 2006, p. 39). It involves both critical work, destabilising accustomed ways of doing and being, and positive work, opening spaces in which it is possible to think and be otherwise. These are modifications in our relation to the present and the different ways in which we are able to recognise ourselves as subjects.

To be clear, and to reiterate, this is 'not a struggle to emancipate some pristine truth from the distortions wreaked upon it by power or ideology, it is not a battle on behalf of truth' (Blacker 1998, p. 358). It is certainly not a revelation of some interior depth. This is not merely a matter of 'denying or resisting truth, power or wealth, but attempting to articulate and deploy them otherwise' (Nealon 2008, p. 95). In arguing against truth an opportunity for the re-articulation of self is created. However, as noted above, by illuminating the limits of self-constitution we do make ourselves vulnerable in different ways. 'We await the ineluctable link between ethical well being and loss of self' (Pignatelli 2002, p. 171), that is we risk facelessness, making ourselves unrecognisable and irrelevant. Indeed, as we attempt self-formation we submit ourselves to 'an experience, then, in which what one is oneself is, precisely, in doubt' (Burchell 1996, p. 30). Over and against this, in Foucault's words, 'a person is nothing else but his relation to truth, and this relation to truth takes shape or is given form in his own life' (Blacker 1998, p. 71).

What I have sought to do in this chapter is to outline Foucault's dispositif of critique, the heretogeneous assembly of concepts, techniques, practices that form a programme for unsettling, for un-educating, for creating spaces in which we might be different. This begins with an attitude, a commitment to curiosity, and what Foucault (1983, p. 14) calls 'a debunking impulse', and ends with violation. But this is not negative and nihilistic, rather it is a positive enterprise and a social one. As Goldstein (1994, p. 15) says:

> There is something in Foucault's very unsettled nature – his famous changes of mind; his alternations between an icily cold, critical eye and shows of passion, between disdain for our old, self-deceptive humanism and attachment to it – that fits the unsettled world in which we write history today.

All of this opens a space of possibility within which we might think education differently. In the following chapter I will look beyond the limits of liberal education to glimpse something different, an experiment with Foucault's tools—and with the help of other writers. This will be a provisional and tentative account of a form of government and of social relations within education built upon capabilities of and a disposition of critique.

References

Allen, A. (2014). *Benign violence: Education in and beyond the age of reason*. Basingstoke: Palgrave Macmillan.

Ball, S. J. (2003). The teacher's soul and the terrors of performativity. *Journal of Education Policy, 18*(2), 215–228.

Bernauer, J. (1987). Michel Foucault's ecstatic thinking. *Philosophy & Social Criticism, 12*(2–3), 156–193.

Bernstein, R. J. (1992). *The new constellation: The ethical-political horizons of modernity/postmodernity,* Cambridge, Mass: MIT Press.

Blacker, D. (1998). Intellectuals at work and in power: Towards a Foucauldian research ethic. In T. S. Popkewitz & M. Brennan (Eds.), *Foucault's challenge: discourse, knowledge and power in education*. New York: Teachers College Press.

Boucher, G. (2006). The politics of performativity: A critique of Judith Butler. *Parrhesia, 1,* 112–141.

Bradbury, A. (2013). *Understanding early years inequality: Policy, assessment and young children's identitites*. Abingdon: Routledge.

Burchell, G. (1996). Liberal government and techniques of the self. In A. Barry, T. Osborne, & N. Rose (Eds), *Foucault and political reason*. London: UCL Press.

Butler, J. (1990). *Gender trouble*. New York: Routledge.

Butler, J. (1995). For a careful reading. In S. Benhabib, J. Butler, D. Cornell, & N. Fraser (Eds.), *Feminist contentions: A philosophical exchange. Thinking gender*. New York: Routledge.

Butler, J. (1997). *Excitable speech. A politics of the performative*. New York & London: Routledge.

Butler, J. (1998). Performance acts and gender constitution. *Theatre Journal, 4*(4), 519–531.

Butler, J. (1999). *The psychic life of power*. Stanford: Stanford University Press.

Butler, J. (2005). *Giving an account of oneself*. New York: Fordham University Press.

Chideya, F. (2015). No child left un-mined? Student privacy at risk in the age of big data. *The Intercept*.

Clarke, M. (2012). The (absent) politics of neo-liberal education policy. *Critical Studies in Education, 53*(3), 297–310.

Davidson, A. (2001). In praise of counter-conduct. *History of the Human Sciences, 24*(4), 25–41.

De Lissovoy, N. (2011). Pedagogy in common: Democratic education in the global era. *Educational Philosophy and Theory, 43*(10), 1119–1134.

Dean, M. (1994a). *Critical and effective histories. Foucault's methods and historical sociology*. London/New York: Routledge.

Dean, M. (1994b). "A social structure of many souls": Moral regulation, government, and self formation. *Canadian Journal of Sociology, 19*(2), 145–168.

Dean, M. (2010). *Governmentality: Power and rule in modern society*. London: Sage.

Defert, D., & Ewald, F. (Eds.). (2001). *Dits et Écrits 1954–1988. Vol. II, 1976–1988 Michel Foucault*. Paris: Gallimard.

Deleuze, G., & Foucault, M. (1977). Intellectuals and power: A conversation. In M. Foucault (Ed.), *Language, counter-memory, practice*. Oxford: Basil Blackwell.

Dreyfus, H. L., & Rabinow, P. (1983). *Michel Foucault: Beyond structuralism and hermeneutics* (2nd ed.). Chicago: University of Chicago Press.

Falzon, C. (1998). *Foucault and social dialogue: Beyond fragmentation*. London: Routledge.

Ferguson, J. (2011). Toawrd a left art of government: From 'Foucauldian critique' to Foucauldian politics. *History of Human Sciences, 24*(4), 61–68.

Foucault, M. (1974). *The archaeology of knowledge*. London: Tavistock.

Foucault, M. (1977a). *Language, counter-memory, practice: Selected essays and interviews*. Ithaca, NY: Cornell University Press.

Foucault,   M.   (1977b).   Powers   and   strategies.   https://static1.squarespace.com/static/
     54889e73e4b0a2c1f9891289/t/565f45d8e4b04361a9e753a9/1449084376295/Michel
     +Foucault+-+Power+and+Strategies.pdf
Foucault, M. (1980a). *Power/knowledge: Selected Interviews and other writings*. New York:
     Pantheon.
Foucault, M. (1980b). Truth and power. In C. Gordon (Ed.), *Power/knowledge: Selected
     interviews and other writings, 1972–1977*. UK: Harvester.
Foucault, M. (1980c). Two lectures. In C. Gordon (Ed.), *Power/knowledge*. London: Longman.
Foucault, M. (1981). *The history of sexuality: An introduction*. Harmondsworth: Penguin.
Foucault, M. (1982a). The subject and power. *Critical Inquiry, 8*(4), 777–795.
Foucault, M. (1982b). The subject and power: Afterword to. In H. Dreyfus & P. Rabinow (Eds.),
     Michel Foucault: Beyond structuralism and hermeneutics. Chicago: University of Chicago
     Press.
Foucault, M. (1983). Discourse and truth: The problematization of Parrhesia: 6 lectures given by
     Michel Foucault at the University of California at Berkeley, October–November 1983.
     Berkeley University. http://foucault.info/documents/parrhesia/
Foucault, M. (1986). *Death and the Labyrinth: The world of Raymond Roussel*. New York:
     Doubleday.
Foucault, M. (1988a). *Politics, philosophy, culture: Interviews and other writings 1972–1977*.
     New York: Routledge.
Foucault, M. (1988b). Power, moral values, and the intellectual. An interview with Michel
     Foucault by Michael Bess. *History of the Present, 4*, 1–2, 11–13.
Foucault, M. (1988c). Truth, power, self: An interview with Michel Foucault. In L. H. Martin, H.
     Gutman, & P. Hutton (Ed.), *Technologies of the self: A seminar with Michel Foucault* (pp. 9–
     15). London: Tavistock.
Foucault, M. (1991). *Remarks on Marx: Conversations with Duccio Trombadori*. New York:
     Semiotext(e).
Foucault, M. (1992). *The history of sexuality Vol. 2: The use of pleasure*. Harmondsworth:
     Penguin.
Foucault, M. (1997a). *Ethics: Subjectivity and truth*. London: Penguin.
Foucault, M. (1997b). What is critique? Translated into English by Lysa Hochroth. In S. Lotringer
     & L. Hochroth (Eds.), *The politics of truth*. New York: Semiotext(e).
Foucault, M. (1998). What is an author. In P. Rabinow (Ed.), *Aesthetics, method, and
     epistemology*. New York: The Free Press.
Foucault, M. (2004). *Society must be defended*. London: Penguin Books.
Foucault, M. (2005). *The hermeneutics of the subject: Lectures at the College de France 1981–82*.
     New York: Picador.
Foucault, M. (2009). *Security, territory, population: Lectures at the College de France 1977–78*.
     New York: Palgrave Macmillan.
Foucault, M. (2013a). *The Will to Know: Lectures at the College de France 1970–71*. London:
     Palgrave.
Foucault, M. (2013b). *The Will to Know: Lectures at the College de France 1983–84*.
     Basingstoke: Palgrave MacMillan.
Foucault, M. (2016). *About the beginning of the hermeneutics of the self: Lectures at Dartmouth
     College, 1980*. Chicago: University of Chicago Press.
Foucault, M. (Ed.). (1997c). *What is enlightenment*. New York: Semotext(e).
Goldstein, J. (1994). Introduction. In J. Goldstein (Ed.), *Foucault and the writing of history*.
     Oxford: Blackwell.
Gulson, K. N., & Webb, P. T. (2016). The new biological rationalities for education policy:
     (Molecular) biopolitics and governing the future. In S. Parker, K. N. Gulson & T. Gale (Eds.),
     Education policy and social inequality, Dordrecht: Springer.
Hartmann, J. (2003). *Power and Resistance in the Later Foucault*. Paper presented at the Annual
     Meeting of the Foucault Circle, John Carroll University, Cleveland, OH.

Hook, D. (2007). *Foucault, psychology and the analytics of power*. Basingstoke: Palgrave MacMillan.

Hunter, I. (1996). Assembling the school. In A. Barry, T. Osborne, & N. Rose (Eds.), *Foucault and political reason: Liberalism, neo-liberalism and rationalities of government*. London: UCL Press.

Koopman, M. (2014). Michel Foucault's critical empiricism today: Concepts and analytics in the critique of piopower and inforpower. In J. D. Faubion (Ed.), *Foucault now: Current perspectives in Foucault studies*. Cambridge: Polity Press.

Lazzarato, M. (2009). Neoliberalism in action inequality, insecurity and the reconstitution of the social. *Theory Culture & Society, 26*(6), 109–133.

Legg, S. (2005). Foucault's population geographies: Classifications, biopolitics and governmental spaces. *Population Space and Place, 11*(3), 137–156.

Lemert, C., & Gillan, G. (1982). *Michel Foucault: Social theory and transgression*. New York: Columbia University Press.

MacIntyre, A. (1990). *Three rival versions of moral enquiry: Encyclopaedia, genealogy, and tradition*. Notre Dame, IN: University of Notre Dame Press.

MacKenzie, I. (1994). Limits, liminality and the present: Foucault's Ontology of Social Criticism Available from Mackenzie. http://limen.mi2.hr/limen1-2001/iain_mackenzie.html

Macleod, C., & Durrheim, C. (2002). Foucauldian feminism: The implications of governmentality. *Journal for the Theory of Social Behaviour, 32*(1), 41–60.

Mahon, M. (1992). *Foucault's Nietzscean genealogy: Truth, power and the subject*. Albany: SUNY.

Marshall, J. (1990). *Michel Foucault: Education and the de-centred self*. University of Aukland.

Martin, L. H., Gutman, H., & Hutton, P. H. (Eds.). (1988). *Technologies of the self: A seminar with Michel Foucault*. London Tavistock.

Mayo, C. (2007). *Disputing the subject of sex: Sexuality and public school controversies*. Lanham, MA: Rowman and Littlefield.

McCarthy, T. (1994). The critique of impure reason: Foucault and the Frankfurt School. In M. Kelly (Ed.), *Critique and power: Recasting the Foucault/Habermas debate*. Cambridge, MA: MIT Press.

Miller, J. (1993). *The passion of Michel Foucault*. London: Flamingo.

Mills, S. (2003). *Michel Foucault,* London: Routledge.

Nealon, J. T. (2008). *Foucault beyond Foucault*. Stanford: Stanford University Press.

O'Farrell, C. (1989). *Foucault: Historian or Philosopher?* London: Macmillan.

Olssen, M. (2003). *Foucault and critique: Kant, humanism and the human sciences*. Paper presented at the British Educational Research Association Annual Conference.

Osborne, T. (2009). Foucault as educator. In M. A. Peters, A. C. Besley, M. Olssen, S. Maurer, & S. Weber (Eds.), *Governmentality studies in education*. Sense: Rotterdam.

Pignatelli, F. (1993). What can I do? Foucault on freedom and the question of teacher agency. *Educational Theory, 43*(4), 411–432.

Pignatelli, F. (2002). Mapping the terrain of Foucauldian ethics: A response to the surveillance of schooling. *Studies in Philosophy and Education, 21*(1), 157–180.

Rabinow, P. (Ed.). (1987). *The Foucault reader*. Harmondsworth: Penguin.

Rabinow, P., & Rose, N. (2003a). Thoughts on the concept of biopower today from LSE. http://www.lse.ac.uk/sociology/pdf/RabinowandRose-BiopowerToday03.pdf

Rabinow, P., & Rose, N. (Eds.). (2003b). *The essential Foucault: Selections from essential works of Foucault, 1954–1984*. New York: New Press.

Ransom, J. S. (1997). *Foucault's discipline: The politics of subjectivity*. Durham, NC: Duke University Press.

Rorty, R. (1986). Foucault and Epsitemology, In D. Hoy (Ed.), *Foucault: A critical reader,* Oxford: Basil Blackwell.

Ross, A. (2008). Why is 'speaking the truth' fearless? 'Danger' and 'truth' in Foucault's discussion of Parrhesia. *Parrhesia, 4*(1), 62–75.

Scott-Baumann, A. (2009). *Ricoeur and the hermeneutics of suspicion*. London: Continuum.

Taylor, C. (1989). Sources of the Self: *the making of the modern identity*. Cambridge, MA: Harvard University Press.

Walzer, M. (1988). The lonely politics of Michel Foucault. In M. Walzer (Ed.), *The company of critics: Social criticism and commitment in the Twentieth Century*. New York: Basic Books.

Youdell, D. (2006). *Impossible bodies, impossible selves: Exclusions and student subjectivites*. Dordrecht: Springer.

Youdell, D. (2011). *School trouble: Identity, power and politics in education*. London: Routledge.

Zembylas, M. (2015). 'Pedagogy of discomfort' and its ethical implications: The tensions of ethical violence in social justice education. *Ethics and Education, 10*(2), 163–174.

Chapter 3
Education as the Pedagogy of the Self

Abstract This chapter takes up the possibility of 'lines of fragility' explored in Chap. 2, in relation to education, through Foucault's later work on subjectivity and 'the care of the self'. It both considers subjectivity as a significant site of political struggle and education and explores some of the techniques of care that Foucault draws upon—from Greco-Roman and early Christian sources—as *a pedagogy of the self*. Drawing on the work of Infinito and others the outlines of a Foucauldian education are sketched. This means recognising students as ethical beings capable of reflection, decision-making and responsibility for their identity and their social relations.

Keywords Care of the self · Self-writing · Parrhesia · Refusal · Transgression

> Nowadays, the struggle against the forms of subjection—against the submission of subjectivity—is becoming more and more important, even though the struggles against forms of domination and exploitation have not disappeared. Quite the contrary. (Foucault 1982, p. 213)

> … critique is the movement through which the subject gives itself the right to question truth concerning its power effects and to question power about its discourses of truth. Critique will be the art of voluntary inservitude, of reflective indocility. (Foucault 1997)

This will be the most difficult chapter to write. It takes up the possibility of 'lines of fragility' explored in Chap. 2, in relation to education, through Foucault's later work on subjectivity and 'the care of the self'. In this later work Foucault suggests that he is seeking to remediate the over-emphasis on domination in his earlier work. Here, following this 'move', I will both consider subjectivity as a significant site of political struggle and education and explore some of the techniques of care that Foucault draws upon—from Greco-Roman and early Christian sources—as *a pedagogy of the self*. As Foucault (Foucault 1987a) put it in an interview 'in order to practice freedom properly, it was necessary to care for the self' and he goes on to say 'the care of the self appears like a pedagogical, moral and also ontological condition for the constitution of a good leader' (p. 124)—an issue to which I will return later as it might pertain to educational relations. Foucault identified two

© The Author(s) 2017
S.J. Ball, *Michel Foucault*, SpringerBriefs on Key Thinkers in Education,
DOI 10.1007/978-3-319-50302-8_3

avenues of the care of the self as the two primary concerns of western philosophy: 'On the one hand, a philosophy whose dominant theme is knowledge of the soul and which from this knowledge produces an ontology of the self. And then, on the other hand, a philosophy as test of life, of bios, which is the ethical material and object of an art of oneself.' (Foucault 2011, p. 127). It is the latter with which he is primarily concerned. He makes a further distinction between pedagogy, what we know or rather what we don't know, and 'psychagogy' the transmission of a truth whose function is not to endow any subject whomsoever with abilities, etcetera, but whose function is to modify the mode of being of the subject to whom we address ourselves' (Foucault 2010a, b, p. 407). That is, who are we or what might we be or become as a speaker of truth? (see http://www.academia.edu/835704/Pedagogy_or_Psychagogy_A_Foucauldian_Distinction). This is an aspect of self-formation, a nexus of truth, life, politics and thinking. This is a dynamic, emergent and unpredictable form of politics. Pedagogy, on the other hand is a planned process in relation to known goals or outcomes, particular skills or abilities.[1] Foucault explained in an interview:

> In the main, political analysis and critique are yet to be invented. [. . .] Which is to say that the problem isn't so much to define a political "position" (which brings us back to making a move on a pre-constituted chessboard) but to imagine and bring into existence new schemas of politicization. If to "politicize" means to bring back to ready-made choices and orga- nizations, all those relations of force and mechanisms of power which analysis disengages, then it's not worth the trouble. (Foucault 1979, p. 72)

Again, as always, Foucault rejects the assumptions of the question to which he responds here and rather calls into question that we which we calls 'politics'. I will return to pedagogy and politics later.

There is a further move in this later writing, that is, a further aspect of the complex relationships between the subject, freedom and truth. Foucault says: '… in order to really care for the self, one must listen to the teachings of a master. One needs a guide, a counsellor, a friend—someone who will tell you the truth' (Foucault 1987b, p. 287). What are we to make of the reappearance here of the teacher and of truth? Again there is an apparatus here we can explore that might enable us to think differently about education—another Foucauldian dispositif if you like (see Chap. 2), that relates psychagogy and pedagogy to the practices of parrhesia and self-formation and 'the politics of the self'—a framework for a Foucauldian education.

> In the 1980s, Michel Foucault and Guattari each followed different paths to arrive at the conclusion that the production of subjectivity and the constitution of the 'relation to the self' were the sole contemporary political questions capable of pointing the way out of the impasse in which we still continue to flounder. Each in their own way they revealed a new dimension irreducible to power and knowledge relations. (Lazzarato Signs and Machines: Lazarrato   (http://anarchistwithoutcontent.wordpress.com/2014/06/10/maurizio-lazzarato-signs-and-machines-introduction/)

---

[1]Which of course have their place in a rounded education.

Speaking Truly: Pedagogy, Psychagogy and Parrhesia

In many respects education is quintessentially an endeavour focused on the question of truth. Truth is at stake in the meaning and practice of education, and what it means to be educated, in a number of senses. I will explore some aspects of truth by returning to email exchanges with some the teachers introduced in Chap. 2. In particular I want to consider Walter, both as a truth-teller and as a site of government, a point of contact between technologies of domination and technologies of the self. More generally thinking about Walter in this way allows us to think about the relations between the subject and truth, as mediated by power. However, Walter will also provide an opportunity to explore the shifts and contradictions and/or continuities between Foucault's emphasis in his early and middle period work on the 'will to truth' and the focus in his late work on truth-telling, and this will also provide a segue into a discussion of self-formation and thence to a final section on what a Foucauldian experience of education might look like or feel like.

In Walter's first school he became embroiled in a complex set of struggles in relation to what it means to be educated, to be a teacher and to teach. These struggles became manifest in a direct engagement with the power relations of contemporary schooling and his engagement in a set of *counter conducts*. These counter-conducts were provoked or made necessary in relation to the practices of government. '[T]he history of the *Raison d'État*, the history of the governmental *ratio*, and the history of the counter- conducts opposed to it, are inseparable from each other' (Foucault 2009, p. 357). Walter seeks to conduct himself in ways different from the institutional attempts to 'conduct his conduct' and as a result of his refusal to be governed that way his *conduct* is identified as unbecoming—as unprofessional.

These counter conducts rest on his discomforts with the role of truth in the school, the truths told about him—in the form of performance reviews and inspections—as a mode by which he is known as an object of measurement. These mechanisms, moments, sites and events are points through which power flows and seeks to produce him as a proper teacher subject. He is brought under the gaze of the state and at the same time he is incited or indeed compelled to 'know himself' properly—to discover and confront his failings and weaknesses and renounce them, and thence to remodel himself as a 'good teacher' (see Moore 2004). The ritual of review and performance management is intended as a kind of purification of the self for the sake of salvation, to bring Walter to the truth of education reform, of 'what works'. These techniques draw, as Foucault argues, on the Christian technology of the confession, an obligation to the truth. He goes on to suggest that those who have sinned, in order to become penitent must 'dramatize' their status. The appraisal meeting provides a site for this dramatization, a ritual manifestation of the truth of oneself—'evil thoughts can be recognized by their tenacious resistance to being verbalised' (Foucault 2016, p. 12). This is a manifestation that Walter refuses and seeks to subvert; although this leads to a disciplinary procedure and ultimately dismissal. The point here is that speaking the truth about oneself also makes, constitutes or constructs forms of one's self, what one is.

Last term I was pretty outspoken during my first 'Performance Management' meeting of the year. This led to a letter from the governors stating: The Governors…wish to convey to you their disappointment in the fact that you were not prepared with all the evidence needed at the initial meeting to make a judgment. It is their expectation that all staff come to meetings ready with all the evidence required so that time dedicated to such meetings can be purposefully used (…) It was noted that some of your comments were not conducive to such a meeting, for example, you stated that 'you did not like being performance managed' (or words to that effect). It is essential that all staff show respect for the processes in the school which secure better outcomes for children. It is the role of leaders in the school to challenge the performance of staff in relation to improving outcomes for children. Respect must be shown for their role. It is expected that your future conduct in such meetings is professional. (Walter)

In the INSET before last we learned about how OfSTED are now looking to 'triangulate' evidence so that how you are judged as a teacher is not just about your performance on the day but involves looking at the results and progress of the children you teach. It's not clear why it took OfSTED twenty years to realise this.

Our headteacher drew attention to the new language of 'In Need of Improvement' that replaces 'satisfactory'. She said that, in a sense, it is meaningless, because even an out-standing teacher is 'in need of improvement'. I would prefer 'we are always learning', a subtle difference but one that cuts to the heart of how we currently define education and learning. (Walter)

I attach a description of an Ofsted inspection of a lesson. It is written by a teacher I met on a course (I am now a primary specialist which I love doing). This teacher read my own description of a bogus observation that I had experienced (I sent you an email about this on Jan 9) and felt compelled to write in detail about her own similar experience. Result: one crushed teacher and one grade produced for the data banks. (Walter)

Here we see truth in a relation of mutual incitement with power. The truth about Walter is embedded in an overlapping discourse of state-authorised pedagogy and school management or leadership that produces a version of teacher professionalism in its image, against which Walter's behavior is judged to be unprofessional. He is in effect cast out from the professional community—as defined by the technologies of government. Discourses and practices of 'evidence', 'observation', 'inspection' and 'improvement' swarm around and produce 'the teacher' in specific ways, and exclude those found wanting. The 'manifold relations of power which permeate, characterise and constitute the social body … cannot themselves be established, consolidated nor implemented without the production, accumulation, circulation and functioning of a … certain economy of discourses. (Foucault 1980, p. 73). In the current context this economy is as real as it is metaphorical. The methods of school 'improvement' are 'borrowed' from businesses practices and the ontology of the school, the teacher and the student, as noted in Chap. 1, is that of the firm—investment in growth related to the expectation of future 'returns' in terms of student performance and employability is the governing rationale for education.

Here also, in Walter's encounter with discourse, again as indicated in Chap. 1, we glimpse an apparatus, a *dispositif of government*, that joins up the micro-management of individual teachers and their practices with the management of the population by the modern state. This joining up is achieved in a very practical and deliberate way via what Barber (2007) calls 'deliverology', the construction of 'the delivery chain', that is hierarchies of 'expectation' that connect the 'front line' service delivery to the responsible minister by ensuring 'sharp focus' on performance priorities (rather than purposes) (see Ball et al. 2011). According to Barber the key elements of deliverology are: the use of good data, setting targets and trajectories, consistent, regular and frequent stock-taking (reporting), figuring out the 'delivery chain', and tracking progress on a regular basis. Through the work of the 'delivery chain' and other facets of contemporary education policy, the productivity and effectiveness of individual teachers is harnessed to the goal of global economic competitiveness (Ball 2008). The social field of education is re-structured as a bio-political project. In relation to this Foucault urges that we ask 'what is the mode of being that this discourse of veridiction imposes on the subject who employs it?' (Foucault 2010a, pp. 309–310). The truths that teachers are encouraged to speak about themselves, and in turn about their students, in and through their performance reviews etc., are connected to normalising, authority-bearing practices. In and through these practices authoritative fictions are constructed and recorded. Subjectivity is thence a key site of government, a point of contact, where truth and power are articulated in the form of practices, to produce a new *effective* teacher subject.

Over and against this *dispositif* of government Walter seeks to question, at the local level, the truth effects of the practices of confession and objectification. In doing so he questions the specific effects of power and articulates a register of the political. 'I say "politically", giving the word "political" a very large meaning' (Foucault 2016, p. 92). As Foucault puts it Walter engages in a 'battle' 'around truth' not on its 'behalf' but about its 'status' and 'the economic and political role it plays' (Foucault 1980, p. 132). This reflects Foucault's concerns; not with defining truth, but with defining its stakes and effects.

In his course at Berkeley in 1983 (Foucault 1983a) and his lectures at the College de France in 1983–4 (Foucault 2011), Foucault took his exploration of truth and its relation to politics in new direction, addressing the practice of *parrhesia*—fearless speech—a final iteration of his interest in 'games of truth'. He re-focused attention from truth to the truth-teller, and to truth-telling as an activity. Drawing on his close reading of Greek and Roman texts and the role of *parrhesia* in Athenian political liberty, Foucault explores truth-telling as a way for forming and testing oneself as a subject. This is the shift, the adjustment of focus and purpose, that is first evident in the move from *Discipline and Punish,* which explores the instituting and perfection of modernity in the form of the prison, and in which humans are positioned as objects of knowledge and of classification, to the *History of Sexuality*, which considers the ways in which, through speaking 'truthfully' in relation to power, we make ourselves as political subjects. This is another point where the question of discontinuity in Foucault's work arises (see Ross 2008). In an interview in 1984 (Foucault 1997), the year of his death, Foucault explained the change in his thinking about the relations of subjectivity and truth. In his earlier thinking he had conceived of the relationship between the subject and 'games of truth' in terms of either coercive practices (psychiatry or prison) or theoretical-scientific discourses (the analysis of wealth, of language, of living beings, especially in *The Order of Things*). In his later

writings he moves to an emphasis on games of truth not as a coercive practices, but
rather as *an aesthetic practices of self-formation*. 'Aesthetic' in this context meaning
an 'exercise of self upon the self by which one attempts to develop and transform
oneself, and to attain a certain mode of being' (Foucault 1997a, p. 282).

However, it is important to recognise the status of his later lectures, they represent a set of openings, possibilities and tools, not an analytic or fully worked
through philosophical programme. They are incomplete and initial forays, curtailed
by Foucault's death. They are 'work in progress, and it is not certain when or even
if the work will be conclusive—or to what degree it has even begun' (Kromann and
Andersen 2011, p. 230)—as always he is 'continuously analysing, developing and
displacing concepts' (p. 230). Nonetheless, in these late works Foucault seems to
suggest a continuity between this preoccupation with the enlightenment and critique
and his interest in the practices of truth telling (see Foucault 2001). The latter is
presaged by and extends his earlier consideration of critique and the critical attitude
and the 'philosophical life' in his discussion of Kant[2] and the Enlightenment. The
last two sets of Foucault's lectures are also different from his earlier work in the
sense that they are less analytic and genealogical, but they do have some divergent
continuities with his previous concerns, in particular with regard to the on going
focus on the relations of truth, government and subjectivity—what he calls in this
case, three poles: 'the pole of aletheia and truth-telling; the pole of politeia and
government; and finally the pole of what, in late Greek texts, is called ethopoiesis'
(the formation of ethos or of the subject) (Foucault 2011, p. 66).

> Modern critique is, Foucault argues, originally and essentially critique and resistance of a
> way of being governed, and also, if not invariably, an argument for being governed
> otherwise, or less, or conceivably not at all. In his 1983 lecture, Foucault situates Kant's
> view of Enlightenment as a reconfiguration of the relation between the government of self
> and the government of others. But how to be governed is, as we have seen, the educational
> subject par excellence (my emphasis). Foucault's reflections on the status of the intellectual,
> which evolve into his investigations of truth-telling and the truth-teller, and are continu-
> ously linked to his Kantian thematic of Enlightenment as the problematisation of the
> present, are nor unrelated to this focal location of the public critical and intellectual function
> at the point of contact of the governmental and the educational. (Gordon 2009, p. xxi)

In the last works Foucault also begins to speak about the ethical value of truth.
There is perhaps, in a rather grand sense, the deployment of his oft used trope of
reversal, in as much that points of contact, sites of government, come to be
opportunities to confront and contest power with 'truth' and to take up the possibility of self-formation. This is significantly different from his earlier work on the

[2]Kant himself was opposed to the total state control of schools (and called for a regime allowing
for experimentation in schooling) because it is liable to impede the educational task of enlightenment: he said 'we are met by two difficulties—parents usually only care that their children make
their way in the world, and Sovereigns look upon their subjects merely as tools for their own
purposes. Parents care for the home, rulers for the state. Neither has as their aim, the universal
good and the perfection to which man is destined, and for which he has also a natural disposition.
But the basis of a scheme of education must be cosmopolitan' (Kant 2012, p. 15—*On Education*,
Dover Publications, Mineola, New York).

relationships between truth, power and expertise in the disciplines and psy-sciences. Ross (2008, p. 69) suggests that 'More specifically, I think he articulates truth as an ethical practice in the form of an explicit alternative to the practices of the disciplines and the particular role that knowledge and the fiction of interior depth play as a stimulant for such practices'.

Parrhesia or Truth-telling, or fearless speech, according to Foucault rests on four criteria or characteristics:

- The speaker makes it manifestly clear what he believes, a frankness, a clarity of belief that 'expresses his personal relationship to truth' (Foucault 2001, p. 19). That is, 'He says what he knows to be true' (p. 14).
- The moral quality of the teller. That is, 'the moral courage of the *parrhesiastes* is evidence of his sincerity, for there is a clear danger in telling the truth' (Peters 2003, p. 212)—an 'ethics of risk'.
- The duty to tell the truth. An ethical characteristic of the good citizen. 'No one forces him to speak, but he feels that it is his duty to do so'. (Foucault 2001, p. 19).
- Truth telling as a form of criticism. '*Parrhesia* is not to demonstrate the truth to someone else, but has the function of *criticism:* criticism of the interlocutor or of the speaker himself (Foucault 2001, p. 17).

This is about disclosing thoughts, not holding back, it is candour without rhetoric, speaking truth to power, always with an element of danger. Within the ideals of Greek democracy this was fundamental to political life and rested on critical assessment, civic duty, and free institutions. 'To be unable to use parrhesia was to have a "slaves mouth"' (Scott 1996).

To reiterate, Foucault here is interested in the *status* of the speaker and the stakes and effects of these practices, and their ethical value, not the definition of truth itself, not what is spoken, but how. *Parrhesia* involves speaking boldly in the face of risk or danger, speaking plainly when there is a difference in power between the speaker and listener, speaking frankly even when it flies in the face of the prevailing discourses and common sense. In this way, through speech, the governed addresses the governing.[3] This boldness is founded on a willingness to criticize, not just social conditions, 'intolerable and catastrophic realities' as Burchell calls them (1996, p. 31), but oneself, indeed especially oneself. Fundamentally, it is the relation to oneself that is important, a shaping of the will—a different kind of 'will to truth'. The *parrhesiates* are also exemplars, and they do not aim to persuade but to tell. Their speech is not assertion but refusal and critique, a confrontation of the normative with the ethical—a challenge to the normalizing truths of the grey sciences. Foucault values truth-telling as an agonistic practice not a normative one. It is the 'relationship between the speaker and what he says' (Foucault 2001, p. 12) that is

---

[3]Of course this begs many questions about the content of fearless speech and its relation to personal or social harmfulness and the freedom of others.

important here, as is the situation, the context of telling. The guarantee of truth is the possession of certain *moral* qualities.

> In this framework, *parrhesia* would not only be truthful engagement with others, but the constructive telling of fictions to both oneself and others that would produce the effects of truth. In this way, *parrhesia* would function proleptically[4] within an aesthetics of existence to modify existing relations of power and to imaginatively construct novel selves and social configurations. (Simpson 2012, p. 100)

There are tools here for thinking about Walter's situation. Walter in his encounters within government and normalising judgements is in effect 'inventing new rules for the game of truth' (Burchell 1996, p. 33), rules in relation to which he conducts himself, at the same time he is highlighting the contingency of practices. He will not submit himself to this technique of government and mounts a criticism of the system of truth to which he is subject—as in his refusal of the terms on which he was performance managed. He is unwilling to speak of himself in terms of this regime of truth and the version of teaching and learning it articulates but instead speaks against it. He does this directly in his school both in his performance review meeting and CPD sessions and then takes his truth speaking into other arenas (his blog) and speaking at events—which brings him directly in relation to questions of democracy.

> I now have a blog: http://jennycollinsteacher.wordpress.com/
>
> It is under a pseudonym as you can see. I have taken the liberty of quoting a number of your works without first asking your permission (see October 13 'Reflections on the New Public Management Systems'). As a fan of Breaking Bad I am glad to see that my pseudonym in your essay is Walter.
>
> This website looks pretty basic and there's not much there at the moment but I hope that, with a broad definition of 'democratic', it will eventually serve to inform people (parents, teachers and pupils) of alternatives to the 'dominant discourse' in education.
>
> I've been greatly enjoying reading Paulo Freire recently.
>
> It's good to hear from you Stephen, Yes you did send me a copy of the Parrhesia paper. I quoted from it in my rant/talk. Like a true amateur public speaker I managed to use 58 min of the 60 min total, leaving 2 min for questions and discussion! Nonetheless I had some good feedback on the day. Something that came out of the whole conference for me is a connection with a new website/network based around ideas of democratic education: http://www.democraticeducation.co.uk/

I think it can be argued that as a speaker Walter is frank, moral, and sincere and clearly risk taking. He is converting shame into courage; as Pignatelli (1993, p. 173) reminds us: 'This is a matter of speaking truth to a form of power which remains deeply embedded in how we understand and assign value to ourselves'. Walter is re-examining himself, or his relation to himself, through this confrontation with risk and refusal, and in relation to prevailing discourses.

---

[4]That is, the anticipation of possible objections in order to answer them in advance.

Dear Stephen,

> I am attaching a letter that I plan to include with my own annual 'Staff Questionnaire'. It is an attack on the relatively new system of insisting on an Ofsted grade for every termly lesson observation. I have used some of your writing about 'Performativity' as a lengthy quote at the beginning. (Walter)

Walter is resisting practices, confronting power in the most immediate sense, very much within Foucault's conception of power; nicely and aptly expressed by Nealon as 'a series of local, sometimes crazy (but still rational, all-too-rational) schemas, deployed almost blindly, certainly experimentally, with no central organising principle' (Nealon 2008, p. 99). All of this relates to the 'specificity of the politics of truth in our societies' (Foucault 1980, p. 132). Walter, and Nigel and Martin (see Chap. 2), are challenging 'the ensemble of rules according to which the true and the false are separated and specific effects of power attached to the true' (Foucault 2010b, p. 407). This is expressed as, and is maybe a good example of, what Foucault writes of as 'the will to discover a new way of governing oneself through a different way of dividing up true and false' and which he also calls 'political spirituality' (Foucault 1980). It is the moral status of speakers which is of primary concern. 'It is not that what the *parrhesiates* sees is invisible to others, it is not the case that "truth" is recalcitrant, but that others choose not to see it' (Ross 2008, p. 71). Walter and his peers as Pignatelli (1993, p. 158) puts it, are 'taking up the challenge of creatively and courageously authoring one's ethical self'. Walter is refusing the truths told about him and his colleagues and confronting the anonymity of power and in doing so is seeking ways to 'care for himself'. In relation to all of this Foucault stresses both the openendedness of the present as a project and freedom as a process of struggle. Freedom is the capacity and opportunity to participate in one's self-formation, and ethics is the practice of this capacity in relation to oneself and others. Freedom is constantly produced and ethics is an ongoing set of practices. 'Foucault's reasoning suggested that bringing about positive, creative, productive human freedom depends on how we act with others, as well as whom we wish to be in relation to those others and in the world' (Infinito 2003, p. 157).

As made clear in the previous chapter, this is not a *positive* ethics, not a matter of asserting ideals, but rather an aestheticism—an imaginative creativity. This is ethics as a practice rather than a plan, as 'the kind of relationship you ought to have with yourself…' (Foucault 1984). It is the cultivation of a self that is both a product and a disruption of various discourses that requires one to practice the art of living well. It is creating a space within which it is possible to make oneself thinkable in a different way—'to become other than how you find yourself' (Foucault 1983b). The teachers I have quoted are utilising their and other's knowledge, their competences and their relation to truth 'in the field of political struggles' (ibid., p. 128). They are not 'rhapsodist[s] of the eternal' (p. 129) but 'hyperactive pessimists' situated in local and immediate fields of struggle. Critical reflection is not enough. As Dilts (2011, p. 143) explains this 'requires us to think not just about how to resist the use of power, but how to conduct ourselves under those rules'. It is about where you stand and what you do today, now—a provocation to respond and to engage in and develop the arts of misconduct.

The role of the *parrhesiates* rests on the choice of a specific relation to oneself. Truth-telling is not simply or even primarily political in the normal sense, it is ethical. The exemplar chooses a relation to themselves that 'may well chart an alternative path for forms of existence to the paths of practices elaborated and reinforced by the normalising tendencies of the disciplines' (Ross 2008, p. 68). This is the choice for self-formation, for a *stylisation* of the self, a care for the self[5]: 'one must care for the self in order to *be* a self' (Infinito 2003, p. 156). To reiterate, this is not a matter of 'knowing the self' but rather the formation of an art of living, or here an art of teaching. Something like what Nietzsche called an *admirable self;* that is 'to give style to one's character' (*The Gay Science*), or what Taylor (1989) calls 'radical reflexivity', opening up the possibility of a different kind of relation to ourselves - to know and to exceed. Audacity is required in initiating this project of self-formation, to achieve a 'delight in oneself' (Foucault 1990, p. 66), in achieving self-mastery—an *askesis*—a practical art of living. This involves establishing, for oneself, a set of correct ways of behaving, against which one judges oneself. 'It is the experience of how one experiences oneself' (Townley 1995, p. 284). Again, it is not self discovery: 'The self has, on the contrary, not to be discovered but to be constituted, to be constituted through the force of truth' (Foucault 2016, p. 37). This is very different from and indeed opposed to some kind of grand design for a new world of experience, it is rooted in local situations and specific incidents—like those described above. It is about the relation between knowing and acting, rather than some kind of inner state or planned alternative. Self-formation is an active and engaged process, based on learning from the immediate and quoditian, forming and testing at the same time; an 'exercise of oneself in the activity of thought' (Foucault 1992, p. 9) over and against or redeploying the techniques of *governmentality*. This brings into play other sorts of 'techniques'. There is a dynamic interplay here between what it is one does not want to be and what one might become. Niesche and Haase (2010, p. 277) in their discussion of the ethics and emotions of becoming an ethical educator, 'see "ethical work" as a dynamic and continuing activity rather than an adherence to a system of moral codes and principles enshrined in formal policy statements'. The task is:

> to effect by their own means or with the help of others a certain number of operations on their own bodies and souls, thoughts, conduct and way of being, so as to transform themselves in order to attain a certain state of happiness, purity, wisdom, perfection, or immortality. (Foucault 1988a, b, p. 18)

One means of such self constitution, Foucault suggests, is the technique of *self-writing*. This is one of 'the arts of oneself' or the government of the self. A deliberate, self-conscious attempt to explain and express oneself to an audience within which the individual exists and seeks confirmation (see Peters 2000). This is, 'Writing as a personal exercise done by and for oneself is an art of disparate truth'

---

[5]This term of used to in the modern sense of style but the Greek meaning, as a matter of artisanship, work done to produce and refine an object using specific skills.

(Lawlor and Sholtz n.d.) or as Deleuze stresses 'to write is to struggle and resist, to write is to become, to write is to draw a map' (Deleuze 1992, p. 44). This seems particularly apt here. Walter's blog, Martin's thesis and Nigel's conference papers and book ideas (see below) are all forms of writing which work from and on a set of institutional circumstances.

> Here's a recent piece of mine. What I want is to have my professionalism restored to me, a culture of formative enhancement, and to continue as a reflective practitioner – as I was, and which was working so superlatively well, but it can't be 'how-gooded'.

> I've a book in me – based on my major report to our inspections review (Nigel)

Such writing 'also constitutes a certain way of manifesting oneself to oneself and to others' (Foucault n.d.), something which again seems evident for these teachers. The emails used and referred to here may also play their part in these 'arts of the self'. Technologies of the self are not enacted in a vacuum, but always within a web of human relations of mutuality and sociality. Again Foucault notes; 'the reciprocity that correspondence establishes is not simply that of counsel and aid; it is the reciprocity of the gaze and the examination' and aptly; 'The writing that aids the addressee arms the writer' (Foucault n.d.). Here writing, reading and responding changes the correspondents and 'nourishes and shapes' them (Weisberger and Butler 2016, p. 1341). As Weisberger and Butler suggest, in relation to digital writing: 'Rather than projecting the already existing self into an online space with the help of social technologies, the self is created as much a posteriori as it exists a priori' (p. 1353). In a similar way writing this book is part of my own self-formation and self-care and it is written over and against education policy, neoliberal higher education and what it is that I have become (Ball 2015). As O'Farrell (2005, p. 118) explains, this is how Foucault came to understand his own writings, as 'experiences' which changed him as he worked on them and which were 'offered as open invitations to the public to have their own experience while reading them'.

> I wrote a paper enclosed where I quoted you. So thanks for helping me stay sane. But your thinking does not permeate our audit-managerial monolith. The effects are dire—harming the real job to an extreme degree, and undermining confidence in the service so that parents are at our throats. They are confused by a mismatch of rhetoric, reality and expectation and here it is descending into a mire of confusion and despondency … (Nigel)

In the examples above we can see Walter and Nigel's attempts to write themselves differently in relation to neoliberal education policy, and its technologies of the self, and Nigel's efforts to articulate himself in concepts set over and against those which hail him through the measurements and categories of performance. Nigel talks of an 'individual's connections to learning and insight (that) literally build new knowledge' and Walter refers to 'intuitive experience and enjoyment' and being 'much less conscious of "Learning Intention" and target-driven and much more built around fun and unconscious development of the whole person'. This is a practice of agonism, an attempt to wrest self-formation from the techniques of government and to make themselves intelligible in different terms. This is also an insurrection of subjugated knowledges[6]—a different version of the teaching subject articulated in a different language—a version of Bulter's *re-description* at work—'the act and strategy of disavowal' (1988a, b, p. 530). In a similar vein, Wain (2007, p. 168) says of Nietzsche: 'Self-creation-education-ethics becomes a matter of self re-description, of re-describing oneself in terms of an ironist vocabulary to which the notion of contingency is central'. We write ourselves as something we are not yet, and may come to disavow. We might even think about Walter's bogus classroom observation (above) as a counter 'dramatization' (Foucault 2016, p. 9)—the 'staging' of a different status, a rejection of penitence by, as Judith Butler puts it, *openly displaying* his own interpretation of good teaching as a re-enactment of norms. The role of the writer Foucault argues is:

> … to see how far the liberation of thought can make … transformations urgent enough for people to want to carry them out and difficult enough to carry out for them to be profoundly rooted in reality. It is a question of making conflicts more visible… Out of these conflicts, these confrontations, a new power relation must emerge, whose first, temporary expression will be a reform. (Foucault 1988b)

All of this opens up 'a non-negative means of relating to oneself'—caring for oneself as a positive fashioning of subjectivity—a version of power that does not merely dominate but 'incites us to forge our own subjectivities within a problematic field, or a field of possible actions and capacities' (Hartmann 2003, p. 10). Casarino and Negri (2004, p. 165) comment, with some degree of license, that 'In the end, Foucault rediscovers and reformulates an old truth, namely that human beings make, build and produce themselves. What emerges in the late Foucault is a humanism after the end of Man'.

What Foucault is doing here, with his constructivist conception of truth, is to see instances of resistance and refusal and indeed truth itself as produced creatively and intentionally. The truths spoken by the *parrhesiastes* are useful and productive fictions with a dual purpose. They function both as a critique of power and circumstance—that is, they are diagnostic—and as a way of narrating the speaker differently—that is they are hermeneutic. By creating dissonance they suggest a future that might be different. 'These fictions serve as "invitations" to change something about the world and are to bring about a "transformation of contemporary man with respect to the idea he has of himself"' (Simpson 2012, p. 105). Critique and self-fashioning are tied together in a form of dialectic. By de-stabilising the subject positions produced for us by technologies of government, we can 'contract

[6]Foucault suggests two forms of 'subjugated knowledges'. One is that of erudite knowledges that have been displaced from or written out of history. The other is local, popular knowledges that are denied a hearing in the spaces of government. The knowledges to which Walter and Nigel refer have elements of both. They both draw from and find inspiration, ways of articulating a different sense of teaching and learning from educational theories that are neglected or excluded from contemporary policy discourses, but blend or intersect these with classroom experience and practice that speak against policy, that gesture to different kinds of classroom relations and different kinds of relations to curricula knowledge.

out' of them and produce different fictions, different relations between self and society. We can author ourselves; as Dean puts it: 'the problem of government cannot be dissociated from a reflection on the relation of individuals to themselves' (Dean 1994, p. 179). Thus, this is a very practical and immediate form of politics that operates both 'in here' in relation to what we have become, and 'out there' in relation to the tools and techniques of government that have made us what we have become.

> Maybe our problem is now to discover that the self is nothing else than the historical correlation of the technology built in our history. Maybe the problem is to change those technologies. (Foucault 2016, p. 76)

In this respect, over and against the vicissitudes of neoliberal education, Walter and Nigel seek to conduct themselves differently, to forge an aesthetics of teaching, of *being* a teacher, and to loosen the connection between subjectification and subjection. This involves new kinds of relations to themselves, their colleagues and their students. They are playing 'games of truth in the relationship of self with self, and the forming of oneself as a subject...' (Foucault 1981, p. 11). These are 'counter-conducts' which open possibilities for the formation of oneself, and for the exercise of philosophy as a means 'to learn to think differently'. This is a politics of refusal.

There are two refusals or a double refusal here, and concomitantly two forms of risk. The first refusal is again double headed, it is a disengagement or renunciation of our 'intelligible' self and a willingness to test and transgress the limits of what we are able to be, a constant engagement with 'what it would mean to exceed or go beyond oneself' (Pignatelli 2002, p. 166), and at the same time a renunciation of the comforts of a transcendental self and the belief that we can know ourselves in some way authentically. The second refusal, implicit or explicit, is of the categories and norms (and measures and judgements) that seek to represent us. It is a rejection of comparison and improvement and indeed of excellence—as currently articulated. That is, the 'moving outside of, resisting, averting these gridded, measured spaces or, at least, diluting their power—is an ethical (as well as political matter)' (Pignatelli 2002, p. 173). The task here is that of 'detaching the power of truth from the forms of hegemony ... within which it operates at the present time' (Foucault 1980, p. 133). The first form of risk is that engendered by 'the perils of self-examination' (Pignatelli 2002, p. 169), the rigors and discipline of uncertainty and unsettledness, an acceptance that 'there is little possibility of ideological and hegemonic closure, no relief from the incessant tensions and contradictions that inform one's identity' (Giroux 1994) and the possibility at the same time that we render ourselves unrecognisable to our colleagues and even in some ways to ourselves. We confront the openness of an unfilled space. This arises from the avoidance of fixity and rather the continuous responsibility to choose ourselves through what we do, and through our practices. This involves 'Tak[ing] oneself as object of a complex and difficult elaboration' (Foucault in Giroux 1994). The second kind of risk is that of exposing ourselves to censure or ridicule or marginalisation—which both Walter and Nigel have experienced.

However, as Olssen (2007, p. 207) makes clear 'Ethical action is not, for Foucault, an individual affair but presupposes a certain political and social structure with respect to liberty'. This is not a lonely narcissism (see criticisms of Butler refered to in Chap. 2). The 'care of the self' Olssen argues is set against the performative individualism of modernity and rests in contrast on what he calls 'thin' communitarianism, which 'has no common goal or bond but comprises of a min-imal structure of argreements, rules, practices, and understandings necessitated to permit a social ontology of difference' (Olssen 2009, p. 489) and he goes on to say 'freedom, in this sense, is a historically and politically constructed space' (p. 491). Thus, 'far from being a lonely and selfish process, self-care fosters generosity and solidarity, enables stronger and more meaningful ties with others' (Sicilia-Camacho and Fernández-Balboa 2009, p. 455). Care of the self is 'operative practice' (Connolly 2008), educator and students 'can enter these practices of freedom to the degree that they become active subjects that display their game within a particular field of relations of knowledge and power' (Sicilia-Camacho and Fernández-Balboa 2009, p. 451).

In another sense of community and the relation to the other, Walter's blog, and his and Nigel's conference papers are attempts to address and hail others who might want to think differently about the possibilities of education and of themselves as teachers. Another of my teacher interlocutors, Chris, sent an interesting email exploring some of the problems and very immediate and pratical dilemmas that might be faced in taking 'care of the self' in relation to others.

> The idea of exploring the limits to which one might 'take care of oneself' by abandoning the discourse of excellence is interesting, exploring what these limits are would be of interest to me, especially the potential contradictions around how 'taking care of oneself' might unwittingly lead to harming others. For example, one might choose to resist (legit-imately) by limiting one's working hours - but if one is required to produce a certain amount of assessment data this could mean that one's lessons become more oriented to teaching to the test and less creative/exploratory (more targeted-selves) as one 'does what the system demands must be done' in lessons, while one's human-relations with other staff might also suffer as one shelves lunch-times in order to leave earlier (more disembedded individualisation), while another strategy - taking risks with students' results by being less syllabus-driven and more expansive in one's content, could just mean reproducing class-inequality, as the middle-classes are always going to be more likely to get help with their exams. Of course if one takes it to the extreme, lip-service to performativity will eventually lead to such a resistor getting the sack.

Another interlocutor, Matthew, based in the US, explained some of the decision-making involved in a change of job and the work of re-fashioning prac-tices and himself, and the ironies and paradoxes he inhabits.

> I'm heading up a team of assessment coaches, a team of professional development trainers, and a small team of people who maintain the current system of measuring student growth (a failing system, frankly). One of our goals is to build teachers' capacity to create their own valid and reliable assessments and make informed decisions with the results.

> There's a great deal of irony in this, as you know very well how I feel about the mea-surement craze and all things neoliberal. The good news, however, is that when I inter-viewed, I was extremely clear about my values – and I've been forthcoming about them

since my first day on the job. So, this may be a great opportunity in what seems to be a flexible urban school district to promote an agenda of re-professionalizing teachers.

These examples point up some of the possibilities and difficulties of an active reconstruction of the relation between government and self-government. If subjectivity is the key site of neoliberal government, the production of particular sorts of 'free' ethical subjects—striving, enterprising, competitive, choosing, responsible—then it is here also, in 'our relation to ourselves' that we might begin to struggle to think about ourselves differently. Ethics becomes the focus of resistance as 'the conscious practice of freedom' (see Nealon 2008, p. 75). As Dilts (2011, p. 132) points out, Foucault was insistent that thinking about 'the subject constituted as practices works both within and against neo-liberal subjectivity and neo-liberal conceptions of freedom, truth, and reality'.

The 'Education of the Soul' (Foucault 1983a)—Education as Self-formation

Can we do more with this Foucauldian *dispositif* of self-formation? Can we think further and differently, with the tools adumbrated above, about what it means to be educated and what it means to be an educator? I want to finish my consideration of Foucault as an educator with some half formed thoughts, some abutments and strings of dots, related to how the intensification of social relations outlined above might relate to and transform what we mean by education. What does self-formation suggest for a different kind of education 'as a space of concrete freedom'? Indeed, Wain (2007, p. 167) says 'For both Nietzsche and Foucault, ethics as the work one does on oneself, and education, are one and the same thing'. However, it is clear if one looks across the whole gamut of philosophical engagements with Foucault's later work that there is no coherent model of education or pedagogy or mastery to be found in his later texts and interviews. Indeed, there is a great deal of incoherence and paradox. What I will do is to follow some possibilities, some lines of flight—creative and resistant possibilities—that Foucault's disruptions enable. James Marshall, who also picks up on Foucault's hints and traces to suggest that education and pedagogy[7] are at the heart of self-formation, says:

> Difficult to envisage in practice, all of this has to be created by experiment. This is an open-ended process, ethical self-formation and future making have no end, no conclusion, and they are contextual – education would be one of many sites in which the subject is in struggle and contingent – not existential. Thus Foucault sought a non-manipulative education where power relationships were minimized, but how this was to be achieved in practice is far from clear, especially in his own teaching. (Marshall 1990, p. 10)

---

[7]The use of the term pedagogy will be a problem from now on, given Foucault's distinction between *pedagogy* and *psychagogy* referred to earlier but I will stick with it.

As Leask (2011) argues the focus on the practices of education in the later Foucault means 'that, instead of being rendered into factories of obedient behaviour, schools or colleges can be the locus for a critically—informed, oppositional micro-politics. In other words: the power-relations that (quite literally) constitute education can now be regarded, on Foucault's own terms, as being creative, "enabling" and positive' (p. 57). So I want to explore now the possibility of some kind of relationship between self-formation and education. That is, the possibility of thinking about or re-thinking education in ways that respond to Foucault's question 'how could it be possible to elaborate new kinds of relationships to ourselves" (Berkeley Lecture 1). (U-Tube). Indeed, Butin (2006, p. 371) argues that there is 'a seemingly natural affinity between Foucault's insights—into, for example, power, knowledge, resistance, subjectification—and educational research and practice'. There are traces of an account of education in several of Foucault's later lectures on Greco-Roman 'political' practices, but clearly these do not add up to a coherent programme. He studies the Greeks as a way of thinking differently about the present. The point is not to act like the Greeks but rather to find ways of acting upon ourselves that are relevant to the present time but which enable us to disrupt and produce ourselves differently, and perhaps in order to do so develop or borrow 'technologies of the self' that enable us to become critical, creative and imaginative in the 'care of the self'. The point of the practices Foucault recovers from the Greeks was to develop 'an attitude, a mode of behaviour; it became instilled in ways of living, it developed into procedures, practices and formulas that people reflected on, developed perfected and <u>taught</u> (my emphasis). It thus came to constitute a social practice, giving rise to relationships between individuals, to exchanges and communications, and at times even to institutions' (Foucault 1987a, p. 45). Indeed:

> Spiritual exercises were a form of pedagogy designed to teach their practitioners the philosophical life that had both a moral and existential value. These exercises were aimed at nothing less than a transformation of one's world view and personality by involving all aspects of one's being, including intellect, imagination, sensibility and will. In the contemporary world, schools have frequently being seen as an appropriate location for the moral education of young people. (Besley 2005, p. 87)

Education in these terms is <u>a relation (or a set of relations) not an institution</u>, the school as an institution is probably irredeemable as a site of domination, reproduction and normalization, but some kinds of other educational spaces need to be created—the internet might be one such space. The point is that education in the present has become one of the key sites at which the processes of normalization are enacted (see Chap. 1) but could become a locus of struggle for productive processes of self-formation and freedom. *The Care of the Self* and the later lectures are littered with hints and possibilities that might be followed if we are to think about education differently, as self-formation. For example, Foucault described individuals engaged in tutoring one another in self-care and in common exercises such as 'letters to friends', to one's 'private consultants' and 'life counselors' (1990, p. 52). Foucault also highlighted the reciprocity with which aid and instruction were given, noting that the 'functions of professor, guide, advisor, and personal confidant were not always distinct—far from it: in the practice of the cultivation of the self, the roles were often interchangeable' (1990, p. 52). In *Self Writing*, he says 'one always needs the help of others in the soul's labour upon itself'. Education as self-formation involves a fundamental re-signification of the categories of student and teacher, and their interactions, purposes and relations. Besley asks directly 'how Foucauldian philosophical notions of care for the self are relevant to the moral education of young people in secondary schools' (Besley 2005, p. 76) and she considers 'implications for how both the student and the teacher each constitute their selves through their different practices of the self—care of the self, knowledge of self, confession and truth-telling' (p. 77). Peters also suggests that 'Foucault's own life and philosophy and the question of ethical self-constitution that concerned him late in his life … offers great prospects for a rehabilitation of Socratic parrhesia—of parrhesiastical education' (Peters 2003, p. 219). Leask (2011, p. 67) suggests that in Foucault's later work there are possibilities which indicate that pedagogy can be reconsidered not simply as a technique for the manufacture of imposition but as 'the theatre of subject creation, of new "practices of the self", new kinds of relations—especially via continued resistance to domination' (p. 67). This is a political education par excellence, and Leask goes on to suggest that 'Teachers and students alike can now be regarded as creative agents, capable of voluntary and intentional counter-practices…' (p. 67). A small number of authors have offered possibilities for what this might look like in practical terms, with Allan (1999) and Youdell (2011) offering probably the best developed examples that attempt to translate Foucault (and in Youdell's case some others) into what she calls 'a political pedagogy' (p. 59).

Infinito (2003) also suggests a practical way forward in enacting 'a political pedagogy'; she identifies from Foucault's *What is Enlightenment?*, three elements of the 'philosophical ethos' that might be translated into educational practices.[8] They are different aspects involved in work on oneself that might be considered as bases of education as self-formation:

(1) An environment that encourages experimentation

As a framework for educational practice this suggests the need to attend to: the form and nature of the space of education, the setting, its frames and practice, and perhaps even its architecture (all of which raise questions of power). Thus '… it is important to conceptualize and configure the classroom as a space for the ongoing practice of ethical self-construction, and to articulate more fully what it means to educate for ethical self-formation' (Infinito 2003, p. 168). Here the classroom is an ethical space, a political space, a concrete space of freedom. In some ways this has affinities with Arendt's conception of 'political space', but it may not be amenable

---

[8]Infinito goes on to say: 'How these technologies are applied and what they might look like specifically in daily life or in the classroom are important questions that call for further theoretical analysis and practical application, which is beyond the scope of this project' (2003, p. 165).

to her argument for the need for stability and institutionalization. For Arendt[9] a political space is made in the space in-between unique and different others, which opens up in human interactions through words, speech, and action, a space where different meanings and commitments meet under the condition of multiplicity. Also, relatedly, Arendt's conception of *being human*, rests on the necessity of being free in public, of acting and speaking in ways that matter in the public world—*parrhesia*? It follows that public freedom requires spaces where our actions are attended to, considered, and taken seriously enough to merit a response. (I come back to this below). This would be a space in which it would be possible to fail, and in which one and one's views and commitments remain open. A space in which it is always possible to 'start again'.[10]

(2) An awareness of one's current condition as defined by the given culture and historical moment. That is; genealogy as curriculum (question of truth).[11] As Infinito (2003, p. 168) suggests:

> Here, we might imagine a curriculum designed to enable multiple genealogical investigations into many other human constructs and disciplines. Such inquiries would be fueled by the production of our own liberty through the ethical construction of ourselves and others, rather than by a market-driven curriculum or one that, while "liberal" in its content, is aimless in its purpose.

As Wain (2007, p. 173) explains there is a relationship here between perspectivism, a view of knowledge as games of truth, and the ethics of self-creation, as he puts it 'the collapse of objective meaning leaves us free to create our own lives and ourselves'. This is not an abdication of truth but rather a self-conscious engagement in the games of truth. Indeed, this might also involve the recovery of subjugated knowledges and thinking 'tactically about the multiple effects of texts and classroom engagements' (Youdell 2011, p. 69) and drawing out and making 'visible subjugated

---

[9]'This is the possibility of "seeing and being seen", of hearing and being heard. This means that the world as a "stage of appearance" consists of a plurality of viewpoints that, in becoming a "public space" (for the living person) also becomes a place for displaying and revealing the "who" (the actor) who makes himself visible individually with acts and words in real stories, and a theatre of public resonance for the events by means of the "who" (the spectator) who witnesses and judges from all sorts of different perspectives' (Arendt 1958, 50–51, 170–172; Tavani 2013, p. 467).

[10]Arendt's political philosophy has other affinities (and differences) with Foucault - in particular her notion of *natality*, the human capacity of "beginning". This capacity of making new beginnings in the world is for her the fundamental human capacity to be free. Also *plurality* her other key concept, is relevant here. That is, the fact that one is born into a world populated by other people who are different from oneself and who one has to come to terms with. It is the condition in which humans are forced to reveal and communicate their uniqueness in order to facilitate living with each other. Plurality is located within public spaces—and it is only within their borders that action and speech are possible.

[11]Here drawing on the Greeks and Romans the curriculum would extend to include physical exercise, music, sexual habits, matters of diet as means of self-care.

meanings and unsettle and open up to troubling those meanings that inscribe the normative' (p. 69). In this spirit, and drawing on research in schools, Youdell presents a set of detailed and nuanced analyses of texts and classroom interactions that introduce into the classroom 'discourses that have not previously belonged there, validating subjectivities that have been disallowed' (p. 72). At the heart of this Youdell argues, drawing on Butler, is *recognizability*, and the possibility of making 'lives that are viable and livable'—the opening up of possibilities and limits of subjectivity. Youdell (2011, p. 115) goes on to say that this means 'intervening in the intolerable present to make "*that-which-is*" "*no longer that-which-is*" inviting us to imagine becomings that disrupt the intolerable … offering instead moments of the haecceity[12] of "this thing" or "here is"'. This will involve the construction of a context in which the dynamics of power and resistance are made apparent and at the same time validated and the focus of these dynamics is the relation between ethics and freedom—'ethics is the form one gives to the practice of one's freedom' (Wain 2007, p. 163). To reiterate this is not an escape from power but its constant inter-rogation. Here we become free and ethical subjects, we produce ourselves, care for ourselves, by making our experience problematic, by practicing new ways of acting, exploring different kinds of relationships, in and through which we care for others. The self is disrupted and produced. This is 'a form of freedom that only comes into being as we try to form ourselves with and in front of others' (Infinito 2003, p. 162) through self reflection and dialogue and disagreement. Taking liberties with Foucault's sentence we might say that the 'proper task' of education is: 'to define the conditions in which human beings "problematize" what they are, what they do, and the world they live in' (Foucault 1987a, p. 27) or as Lazaroiu (2013, p. 825) puts it 'The key ingredients of Foucault's counter-modernist educational program are the skills of self-governance, the ethical (non-dominating) governance of others and the practice of freedom through self-creation'.

(3) An attitude or disposition to critique; a focus on the production of a particular sorts of dispositions that would be valued and fostered, made explicit (questions of subjectivity)—like skepticism, detachment, outrage, intolerance and tolerance (valuing what Olssen (2009) calls 'difference', the basis of 'thin' community), and audacity and fearlessness.

In pedagogical terms, we are talking about encouraging a certain disposition. Lest we think this a radical notion, we must remember that education is practiced at producing desirable dispositions. A history of the hidden curriculum reveals specific attitudes infusing education at various times, deemed part of its responsibility. While such attitudes were once part of the overt justification of schooling, we have only recently been pressured by educational theorists to come clean about the behaviors and dispositions we systematically (if unintentionally) inculcate. (Infinito 2003, p. 170).

---

[12]Which denotes the discrete qualities, properties or characteristics of a thing that make it a *particular* thing.

This is a commitment to fostering ethical learners with a healthy suspicion of the present, while at the same time being able to acknowledge their own fallibility and to set themselves over and against the prevailing framework of modern education with its carceral forms, its assertion of fixed truths and the production of disposition through a hidden, or more recently not so hidden, curriculum organized around enterprise and character. This means being open to the infinite possibilities for change and a willingness to critique even our own commitments; it means adopting a critical stance that moves between attempts to re-create ourselves and the world. A major requirement and effect here is what Zembylas (2015) and others call a *pedagogy of discomfort*; drawing on what Foucault termed 'the ethic of discomfort'. That is, students and teachers are invited to embrace their vulnerability and ambiguity of self and therefore their dependability on others (Zembylas 2015, p. 170). This would mean:

> never to consent to being completely comfortable with one's own presuppositions. Never to let them fall peacefully asleep, but also never to believe that a new fact will suffice to overturn them; never to imagine that one can change them like arbitrary axioms, remembering that in order to give them the necessary mobility one must have a distant view, but also look at what is nearby and all around oneself. (Foucault 1994, p. 448)

In practice, Felman (1992, p. 53) argues:

> If teaching does not hit upon some sort of crisis, if it does not encounter either the vulnerable unpredictable dimension, it has perhaps not truly taught . . . I therefore think that my job as a teacher, paradoxical as it may sound, was that of creating in the class the highest state of crisis that it could withstand, without "driving the students crazy," without compromising the students' bounds.

This is the groundwork for transgression and transformation, not anesthetizing us, or condemning bad faith, but making it possible to act while making it no less difficult to know what to do: 'transgression allows individuals to peer over the edge of their limits, but also confirms the impossibility of removing them' (Allan 1999, p. 48). The object is to create a space within which it is possible to begin to re-imagine the historically sedimented problem (atizations) and questions through which we address the world, a curriculum within which constitute our present— opening up 'a room, understood as a room of concrete freedom, that is possible transformation' (Foucault 1972, p. 5). Education becomes an exploration of limits, mapping, testing and crossing them when possible. That is, a sequence of moments, openings, spaces in which 'critical learning' is possible—ethical heterotopias, real and unreal, where difference is affirmed, 'a sort of simultaneously mythic and real contestation of the space in which we live'.[13]

As Rabinow and Rose (2003, p. xxvii) explain, Foucault's intention is to problematize manifestations of discomfort in order to 'to open a space for movement without slipping into a prophetic posture'. It becomes important and 'necessary to offer students opportunities to unpack their cherished worldviews and

---

[13]("Des Espace Autres", published by the French journal Architecture/Mouvement/ Continuité in October, 1984: http://web.mit.edu/allanmc/www/foucault1.pdf).

'comfort zones' in order to deconstruct the ways in which they have learned to see, feel, and act' (Zembylas 2015, p. 166). This means recognising students as ethical beings capable of reflection, decision-making and responsibility for their identity and their social relations. It involves what we might call, but in a much stronger sense than normally meant, citizenship education or civic education, but here made the core of the educational process and focussed on what we are and our modes of being.

> Pupils can… be encouraged to do work on themselves which allows them to identify goals, scrutinize the limits to achieving these goals and determine individual or collective actions which either challenge or accept these limits. (Allan 1999, p. 59)

Youdell (2011, p. 128) reflecting on one of her exemplar analyses of political pedagogy, that focuses on the attempt to de-pathologise 'disordered' boys, concludes: 'Perhaps here they are becoming- student and learner, a becoming that transforms student, learner and learning itself'. This reformulation rests on a willingness to struggle against what we do not want to be, and at the same time a willingness to interrogate and contest truth effects, and to address the rules that gives status to truth, and the construction of relations within which such a willingness and such struggles can be 'taught'. That is to say, 'Conceiving of education as an effort to aid individual self-construction is educationally sound, ethically responsive, and politically valuable. (Infinito 2003, p. 171). In the same vein, Sicilia-Camacho and Fernández-Balboa (2009), in their recasting of critical pedagogy in Foucauldian terms, in the context of teacher education for physical education, assert that: 'Our version of CP (critical pedagogy) seeks the construction of personal-pedagogical-political ethics while acknowledging the legitimacy of different 'pedagogical games' and "regimes of truth' (p. 458).

In all of this, education, the teacher and pedagogy are articulated not as skills and knowledges but as the formation of moral subjectivity, a form of politics, and a relation to ethics rather than to truth.

> we suggest that individuals are continuously in the process of turning themselves into ethical beings, capable not only of determining their own behaviours, but also able to challenge and resist the dominant codes and structures of society' (Sicilia-Camacho and Fernández-Balboa 2009, p. 458)

This is not liberation but activation, an enduring engagement in the travails and failures of self-fashioning, experimenting with and choosing what we might be and how we might relate to others, not discovering who we really are. This is also a studiedly anti-institutional education, a form of *de-schooling* (Illich 1971), that recasts resistance and critique into the transformation of process and subject. As Leask (2011, p. 68) says 'The construction of new pedagogical possibilities must be critically informed'. But this is an under-statement, rather pedagogy becomes the practice of critique, learning by opposition, an on going critical insubordination aimed at destabilising truth, rather than learning it, historising excellence and beauty rather than appreciating it—'a commitment to uncertainty' (Gordon 1986, p. 74). This must also rest on and contribute to a form of power relations that are enabling, creative and positive (Leask 2011, p. 68). Pertinently, Illich (1971) notes the irony that schools are allegedly a preparation for participation in a democracy but are run in ways which apply rules and sanctions to children which would not be acceptable to adults. Sicilia-Camacho and Fernández-Balboa argue that this is different from CP, whereas CP is a 'moral process whose goal is the emancipation of others', this is 'a morality *as action*, recognizing individual's capacity to develop alternative "subjectivities" and make appropriate decisions' and they add, reflecting on their own practice, 'we have learned the value of caring for the self both for practicing CP and for living a socially and politically engaged life (2009, p. 458). That is, a shift from morality to ethics',[14] from truth to power. And as Barry, Osborne and Rose suggest this is not simply an 'intellectual exercise': 'Rather what is at stake is the production of a certain kind of experience, a reconfiguring of experience itself' (Barry et al. 1993, p. 6)—that we might name as education. Olssen (2009, p. 267) suggests, drawing on Sen and Nussbaum, that all of this presupposes 'a range of capabilities' that education must develop and he goes on to offer a list of requirements for such an education that to a great extent overlap with those of Infinito.

All of this begs questions about the role of the teacher (or guide, mentor) and the school leader[15]—or whatever we might call them, and the power relations between teacher and student. As Foucault writes, he sees no objection to 'those who know more in a given game of truth' telling another 'what he must do, teach him', the problem in this relationship and interaction is 'to avoid the effects of dominance' (Foucault 1988a). The exercise of power over others is not always bad and as Deacon (2006, p. 184) says 'domination can be avoided or minimised by counter-acting practices of power and by practices of liberty'. The teacher must become what Smith (2006) calls a 'genuine interlocutor'. In *Self Writing*, Foucault quotes Seneca, saying 'The process is mutual; for men learn while they teach'. Thus, a key task for a school community is not only to define for itself the questions that matter but collectively construct acceptable, creative solutions to them, an ethical response. As part of this, teachers must nurture truth-telling. (Pignatelli 2002, p. 174), risk and relish challenges, create a public space where fearless speech is encouraged. This must rest on the relationship, for the teacher as much as the student, between care of the self and the care of others. As Foucault points out in his survey of Greek political thought there is a fundamental relation between governing others and governing the self: 'One will not be able to rule if one is not oneself ruled' (Foucault 1990, p.89). The exercise of political power demands the practice and cultivation of personal virtues.

---

[14]And they go on to assert that in their own attempts to bring such an approach to bear that they 'have learned the value of caring for the self both for practicing CP and for living a socially and politically engaged life' (p. 458).

[15]Pignatelli (2002, p. 174) says that 'The role of the leader in such schools must necessarily transcend managerial competence. The leader sets herself the task of establishing and sustaining the school as a learning community whose members systematically attend to the school's well being'.

> It is the power over self which will regulate the power over others … if you care for yourself correctly i.e., if you know ontologically what you are … then you cannot abuse your power over others. (Foucault 1988a)

Allan (1999) has the most thorough and pertinent discussion of the 'problem' of the teacher in these terms in her book on disability, inclusion and schooling. As she points out in the modern school the professionalism of the teacher readily becomes a vehicle for re-inscribing the limits of disability. 'Teachers' practices, framed within special needs discourses, constructed individuals as passive objects of their professional knowledge, with impairments in need of "fixing"' (p. 71), as was discussed in Chap. 1. Over and against this she refers to Lowson's (1994) deconstructive strategy that invites teachers to pathologize themselves as suffering from PTD (Professional Thought Disorder). That is, 'Teachers and other professionals[16] have ethical work to do on themselves, in order to avoid using experience as "terrorism" on those without it … whilst also facilitating their pupils' ethical work' (Allan 1999, p. 118). All of this, as Youdell (2011, p. 11) aptly puts it, is 'fraught'. Refusing to be a 'proper' teacher (ibid.) means that the teacher puts their subjecthood at risk—as was the case for Nigel and Walter. There are also many loose-ends in this attempt to re-think pedagogy, as Deacon (2006, p. 184) points out practices of liberty in the classroom 'are inextricably intertwined with pedagogical effects of guilt, obligation and verification, and assumptions about degrees of ignorance, dependence on others, legitimate compulsion and achievement'.

In Greek politics the ability to govern was not defined 'as if it were a question of a "profession" with its particular skills and techniques" (1990, p. 91)—which is exactly how we now conceive of the work of the teacher—but depended on ethical work of the self on the self—that is the work of self formation. Niesche and Haase (2010, p. 11) describe this as 'the work one does on one's self to become an ethical professional'. And this is rooted, (as noted previously) not in introspection or abstract principles but in the details of practice, specific incidents, it is dependent on memory. It means to be centred but not self-centred—this requires that the teacher 'act upon himself, to monitor, test, improve and transform himself' (Foucault 1992, p. 28)—to produce himself or herself as an ethical subject. In this sense teaching becomes a site of 'delight in oneself' (1990, p. 65) and of the relation between knowing and acting. The teacher has 'the task of establishing a vital, vibrant public space for truth-telling to occur' (Pignatelli 2002, p. 174). This would mean a constant awareness of and re-working of what it means to be a teacher, what Sicilia-Camacho and Fernández-Balboa call 'bio-pedagogy'. Niesche and Haase discuss this in relation to Andrew, a primary school teacher who constantly works to:

---

[16]In a similar but contrary vein, in a recent essay in *The Boston Review*, Dzur says that democracy is usually thought a political movement and participatory democracy points to public involvement in protests, plebiscites, and public action aimed at governmental change. But democracy may also be thought of as a way of life focused on individualism and respect for the power and judgment of each person. Dzur wonders whether the space of democracy is shifting from governmental to professional institutions? And there is a new kind of democratic professionalism (http://bostonreview.net/author/albert-w-dzur).

Ensure that his exercise of power over others is not an abuse of power and is a moral and
productive exercise of power in the way it encourages students to also care for their own
ethical selves. (2010, p. 7)

The bond between master and disciple is always provisional and circumstantial,
the learner is 'directed to acquire a certain degree of autonomy and self-mastery'
(Foucault 2016, p. 10); not by self-exploration but in response to the master's
discourse, the subject as a locus 'where truth can appear and act as a real force'
(Martin et al. 1988).

In the absence of a master there can be no self-concern, but the position of the master is
defined by the fact that he occupies himself with the self-concern of the person he leads,
who can achieve this for himself. (Foucault 2005, p. 86)[17]

The teacher-student relationship thence becomes a complex partnership, a dialogue (see Falzon in Chap. 2) and a series of experiments based on respect and mutual
care, and mutual development. But this is a partnership that is open to constant
scrutiny and revision—with all the dangers and risks that might involve. This is the
'parrhesiatic contract'—in which both parties speak frankly (Peters 2003). Students
are truth-tellers and parrhesia and self-formation are the interweaving of *bios* (life) and
logos (principle), this is a form of ethics and a set of techniques of living, a concrete
practice of freedom with a focus not on concepts or the abstract or ideal but on
practices 'forms, modes and styles of life' (Rabinow 1987). 'The problems of "an
other world" and "an other life" arise together in a politically engaged life whose
precondition is a break with established conventions, habits, and values' (Maurizio
Lazzarato, Signs and Machines, "Introduction" (https://anarchistwithoutcontent.
wordpress.com/2014/06/10/maurizio-lazzarato-signs-and-machines-introduction/).
The subject is produced in the dynamics of power and resistance, in a process that
Bernauer (1987) names as a 'permanent provocation'. However, as Allan (1999, p. 57)
emphasises, in her discussion of the practices of transgression of six disabled students
in a mainstream school: transgression 'was not a singular act, but had to be constantly
repeated and required vigilance from the pupils' and she goes on to say: 'The kind of
otherness attained through transgression was fragmented, liminal and never complete'. This is, 'The art of living dangerously' (ibid., p. 58). In other words, this is the
care of the self, the work of the 'politics of the self', a continuous practice of introspection, which is at the same time attuned to a critique of the world outside: 'critique
is the movement through which the subject gives itself the right to question truth
concerning its power effects and to question power about its discourses of truth.
Critique will be the art of voluntary inservitude, of reflective indocility'. (Foucault n.d.
). Established patterns are to be challenged in order to ascertain what it is that is no
longer indispensable for the constitution of the self. 'The ethical project which
emerges is to envision one's self constitution as an on going task, an achievement

---

[17]This rests on what are sometimes tortuous and fine distinctions. How does the student recognize
the master? How does he extricate himself from the relationship? I have not the space to explore
these issues here but they need careful consideration at some point in relation to a Foucauldian
education.

requiring artistry in the face of the looming, omnipresent threats to our freedom to invent ourselves' (Pignatelli 2002, p. 165). This is not something we can do alone, and not something that comes easily. Education must become a site of practice and a space in which to acquire the skills and sensibilities of self-creation.

> The practice of freedom as an ethical/aesthetic endeavor must be learned. Thus education, if it is to be a liberal (as in liberating) experience, must recognize its role in the ethical self-creation of individuals. Through a combination of his theory of "care of the self" and his understanding of an "Enlightenment ethos," Foucault provided insight into the role society plays in individual self-formation and the possibilities for education. (Infinito 2003, p. 155–56)

What is shared across the various commentaries and examinations of Foucault's educational manifesto is a sense of possibility and bemusement – exactly that dilemma with which Foucault constantly confronts us, between acting and not knowing what to do—freedom? Freedom is not tautological with liberation, freedom is only possible within concrete struggles over situated values, freedom is historically contingent, we have to give up on the idea that freedom has an end point.

Lysimachus and Melesias 'realise that education is required, but what kind' (Foucault 2011, p. 214).

References

Allan, J. (1999). *Actively seeking inclusion: Pupils with special needs in mainstream schools.* London: Falmer Press.

Arendt, H. (1958). *The human condition.* University of Chicago Press: London/Chicago.

Ball, S. J. (2008). *The education debate: Politics and policy in the 21st century.* Bristol: Policy Press.

Ball, S. J. (2015). Accounting for a sociological life: Influences and experiences on the road from welfarism to neoliberalism. *British Journal of Sociology of Education, 36*(6), 817–831.

Ball, S. J., Maguire, M. M., Braun, A., Perryman, J., & Hoskins, K. (2011). Assessment Technologies in schools: 'Deliverology' and the 'play of dominations'. *Research Papers in Education, forthcoming.*

Barber, M. (2007). *Instruction to deliver: Tony Blair, the public services and the challenge of delivery.* London: Methuen.

Barry, A., Osborne, T., & Rose, N. (1993). Liberalism, neo-liberalism and governmentality: An introduction. *Economy and Society, 22*(3), 265–266.

Bernauer, J. (1987). Michel Foucault's ecstatic thinking. *Philosophy & Social Criticism, 12*(2–3), 156–193.

Besley, T. (2005). Foucault, truth telling and technologies of the self in schools. *Journal of Educational Enquiry, 6*(1), 76–89.

Burchell, G. (1996). Liberal government and techniques of the self. In A. Barry, T. Osborne, & N. Rose (Eds.), *Foucault and political reason.* London: UCL Press.

Butin, D. (2006). Putting Foucault to work in educational research. *Journal of Philosophy of Education, 40*(3), 371–380.

Casarino, C., & Negri, A. (2004). It's a powerful life: A conversation on contemporary philosophy. *Cultural Critique, 57*(Spring), 151–183.

Connolly, W. E. (2008). *William E. Connolly: Democracy, pluralism and political theory*. Abingdon: Routledge.

Deacon, R. (2006). Michel Foucault on eduction: A preliminary theoretical overview. *South African Journal of Education, 26*(2), 177–187.

Dean, M. (1994). A social structure of many souls: Moral regulation, government, and self formation. *Canadian Journal of Sociology, 19*(2), 145–168.

Deleuze, G. (1992). What is a dispositif? In T. J. t. Armstrong (Ed.), *Michel Foucault, Philosopher: Essays translated from the French and German*. London: Harvester/Wheatsheaf.

Dilts, A. (2011). From 'entrepreneur of the self' to 'care of the self': Neo-liberal governmentality and Foucault's ethics. *Foucault Studies, 12*(130–146).

Felman, S. (1992). Education and crisis, or the vicissitudes of teaching. In S. Felman & D. Laub (Eds.), *Testimony: Crises of witnessingin literature, psychoanalysis, and history* (pp. 1–56). New York: Routledge.

Foucault, M. (1972). *The archeology of knowledge*. New York: Vintage.

Foucault, M. (Ed.). (1979). *Interview with Lucette Finas*. Sydney: Ferral.

Foucault, M. (1980). *Power/knowledge: Selected interviews and other writings*. New York: Pantheon.

Foucault, M. (1981). *The history of sexuality: An introduction*. Harmondsworth: Penguin.

Foucault, M. (1982). The subject and power: Afterword to. In H. Dreyfus & P. Rabinow (Eds.), *Michel Foucault: Beyond structuralism and hermeneutics*. Chicago: University of Chicago Press.

Foucault, M. (1983a). Discourse and truth: The problematization of parrhesia: 6 lectures given by Michel Foucault at the University of California at Berkeley, Oct–Nov. 1983. Berkeley University: http://foucault.info/documents/parrhesia/

Foucault, M. (1983b). Why study power: The question of the subject. In H. Dreyfus & P. Rabinow (Eds.), *Michel Foucault: Beyond structuralism and hermeneutics*. Chicago: University of Chicago Press.

Foucault, M. (1984). Neitzsche, genealogy, history. In P. Rabinow (Ed.), *The Foucault reader*. London: Peregrine.

Foucault, M. (1987a). The ethic of care for the self as a practice of freedom: An interview with Michel Foucault by Fornet-Betancourt et al. *Philosophy & Social Criticism, 12*, 112–131.

Foucault, M. (1987b). *Ethics, subjectivity and truth: The essential works of Michel Foucault 1954–1984*. Harmondsworth: Allen Lane, The Penguin Press.

Foucault, M. (1988a). The ethic of the care for the self as a practice of freedom (interview). In J. Bernauer & D. Rasmussen (Eds.), *The final Foucault* (pp. 1–20). Cambridge, MA: MIT Press.

Foucault, M. (1988b). *Politics, philosophy. Culture: Interviews and other writings 1972–1977*. New York: Routledge.

Foucault, M. (1990). *The history of sexuality volume 3: The care of the self*. London: Penguin.

Foucault, M. (1992). *The history of sexuality vol. 2: The use of pleasure*. Harmondsworth: Penguin.

Foucault, M. (1994). For an ethic of discomfort. In J. D. Faubion (Ed.), *Essential works of Foucault, 1954–1984* (Vol. 3, pp. 443–448). New York: The New Press.

Foucault, M. (1997). What is critique?" (L. Hochroth, Trans.). In S. Lotringer & L. Hochroth (Eds.), *The politics of truth*. New York: Semiotext(e).

Foucault, M. (1997a). *Ethics: Subjectivity and truth*. London: Penguin.

Foucault, M. (2001). *Fearless speech*. Los Angeles: Semiotext(e).

Foucault, M. (2005). *The hermeneutics of the subject: Lectures at the College de France 1981–82*. New York: Picador.

Foucault, M. (2009). *Security, territory, population: Lectures at the College de France 1977–78*. New York: Palgrave Macmillan.

Foucault, M. (2010a). *The Government of the self and others: Lectures at the College de France 1982–1983*. Basingstoke: Palgrave.

Foucault, M. (2010b). *The hermeneutics of the subject: Lectures at the College de France 1981– 82*. London: Palgrave Macmillan.

Foucault, M. (2011). *The courage of truth: Lectures at the College de France 1983–84* London: Palgrave Macmillan.

Foucault, M. (2016). *About the beginning of the hermeneutics of the self: Lectures at Dartmouth College, 1980*. Chicago: University of Chicago Press.

Foucault, M. (n.d.). Self-writing. itsy.co.uk/archive/sisn/Pos/green/Foucault.doc. Accessed May 17, 2012.

Giroux, H. (1994). *Dusturbing pleasures: Learning popular culture*. New York: Routledge.

Gordon, C. (1986). Question, ethos, event: Foucault on Kant and Enlightment. *Economy and Society, 15*(1), 71–87.

Gordon, C. (2009). Foreword: Pedagogy, psychagogy, demagogy. In M. A. Peters, A. C. Besley, M. Olssen, S. Maurer, & S. Weber (Eds.), *Governmentality studies in education*. Rotterdam: Sense Publishers.

Hartmann, J. (2003). *Power and resistance in the later Foucault*. Paper presented at the Annual Meeting of the Foucault Circle, John Carroll University, Cleveland, OH.

Illich, I. (1971). *De-schooling society*. London: Calder and Boyers.

Infinito, J. (2003). Ethical self-formation: A look at the later Foucault. *Educational Theory, 53.*

Kant. (2012). *On education*. Meneola, New York: Dover Publications.

Kromann, J., & Andersen, T. (2011). Parrêsia: The problem of truth. *Ephemera (Copenhagen), 11* (2), 225–230.

Lazaroiu, G. (2013). Besley on Foucault's discourse of education. *Educational Philosophy and Theory, 45*(8), 821–832.

Leask, I. (2011). Beyond subjection: Notes on the later Foucault and education. *Educational Philosophy and Theory, 44*(1), 57–73.

Lowson, D. (1994). Understanding professional thought disorder: A guide for service users and a challenge for professionals. *Asylum, 8*(2), 29–30.

Marshall, J. (1990). Michel Foucault: Education and the de-centred self. University of Aukland.

Martin, L. H., Gutman, H., & Hutton, P. H. (Eds.). (1988). *Technologies of the self: A seminar with Michel Foucault*. London: Tavistock.

Moore, A. (2004). *The good teacher*. London: RoutledgeFalmer.

Nealon, J. T. (2008). *Foucault beyond Foucault*. Stanford: Stanford University Press.

Niesche, R., & Haase, M. (2010). Emotions and ethics: A Foucauldian framework for becoming an ethical educator. *Educational Philosophy and Theory, 44*(3), 276–288.

O'Farrell, C. (2005). *Michel Foucault*. London: Sage.

Olssen, M. (2007). Invoking democracy: Foucault's conception (with insights from Hobbes). In M. A. Peters & A. C. Besley (Eds.), *Why Foucault? new directions in educational research*. New York: Peter Lang.

Olssen, M. (2009). *Toward a global thin community: Nietzsche, Foucault and the cosmopolitan commitment*. Boulder, CO: Paradigm.

Peters, M. (2000). Writing the self: Wittgenstein, confession and pedagogy. *Journal of Philosophy of Education, 34*(2), 353–368.

Peters, M. (2003). Truth-telling as an educational practice of the self: Foucault, parrhesia and the ethics of subjectivity. *Oxford Review of Education, 29*(2), 207–224.

Pignatelli, F. (1993). What can I do? Foucault on freedom and the question of teacher agency. *Educational Theory, 43*(4), 411–432.

Pignatelli, F. (2002). Mapping the terrain of foucauldian ethics: A response to the surveillance of schooling. *Studies in Philosophy and Education, 21*(1), 157–180.

Rabinow, P. (Ed.). (1987). *The Foucault reader*. Harmondsworth: Penguin.

Rabinow, P., & Rose, N. (2003). Thoughts on the concept of biopower today from LSE: http://www.lse.ac.uk/sociology/pdf/RabinowandRose-BiopowerToday03.pdf

Ross, A. (2008). Why is 'speaking the truth' fearless? 'Danger' and 'truth' in Foucault's discussion of parrhesia. *Parrhesia, 4*(1), 62–75.

Scott, G. A. (1996). Games of truth: Foucault's analysis of the transformation from political to
    ethical Parrhesia. *The Southern Journal of Philosophy, 34*(1), 97–114.
Sicilia-Camacho, A., & Fernández-Balboa, J. M. (2009). Reflecting on the moral bases of critical
    pedagogy in PETE: Toward a Foucaultian perspective on ethics and the care of the self. *Sport,
    Education and Society, 14*(4), 443–463.
Simpson, Z. (2012). The truths we tell ourselves: Foucault on Parrhesia. *Foucault Studies, 13*
    (May), 99–115.
Smith, D. (2006). *Trying to teach in a season of great untruth: Globalization, empire and the
    crises of pedagogy*. Rotterdam: Sense.
Tavani, E. (2013). Hannah Arendt—Aesthetics and politics of appearance. *Proceedings of the
    European Society for Aesthetics, 5*, 466–475.
Taylor, C. (1989). *Sources of the self: The making of the modern identity*. Cambirdge, MA:
    Harvard University Press.
Townley, B. (1995). 'Know thyself': Self-awareness, self-formation and managing. *Organization,
    2*(2), 271–289.
Wain, K. (2007). Foucault: the ethics of self-creation and the future of education. In M. Peters & T.
    Belsey (Eds.), *Why Foucault? New directions in educational research*. New York: Peter Lang.
Weisberger, C., & Butler, S. H. (2016). Curating the Soul: Foucault's concept of hupomnemata
    and the digital technology of self-care. *Information, Communication & Society, 19*(10), 1340–
    1355.
Lawlor, L., & Sholtz, J. (n.d.). Speaking out for others: Philosophy's activity in Deleuze and
    Foucault. Penn State University.
Youdell, D. (2011). *School trouble: Identity*. London Routledge: Power and Politics in Education.
Zembylas, M. (2015). 'Pedagogy of discomfort' and its ethical implications: The tensions of
    ethical violence in social justice education. *Ethics and Education, 10*(2), 163–174.

Druck:
Canon Deutschland Business Services GmbH
im Auftrag der KNV-Gruppe
Ferdinand-Jühlke-Str. 7
99095 Erfurt